Lucretia Crocker

Methods of Teaching Geography. Notes of Lessons

Second Edition

Lucretia Crocker

Methods of Teaching Geography. Notes of Lessons
Second Edition

ISBN/EAN: 9783337165994

Printed in Europe, USA, Canada, Australia, Japan

Cover: Foto ©Paul-Georg Meister /pixelio.de

More available books at **www.hansebooks.com**

METHODS

OF

TEACHING GEOGRAPHY.

NOTES OF LESSONS.

BY

LUCRETIA CROCKER,
MEMBER OF THE BOARD OF SUPERVISORS,
BOSTON PUBLIC SCHOOLS.

Printed at the Request of the Teachers in Attendance.

SECOND EDITION.

BOSTON, MASS.:
BOSTON SCHOOL SUPPLY COMPANY,
NO. 15 BROMFIELD STREET.
1884.

PREFACE.

The writer of these notes, in responding to an invitation to occupy an hour, on four successive Saturdays, in presenting methods of teaching geography, was embarrassed by the breadth of the subject to be treated in so limited a time. It was necessary to determine what could be done, and what could be omitted. A mere outlining of a plan of study would be neither helpful nor satisfactory. It seemed desirable, therefore, to try to indicate the stages of a progressive course of study, and to present methods of teaching a few important points. The topics selected for fuller treatment were among those that require simple and careful presentation by teachers, in order that the concise statements of the text-books may be comprehended by pupils. It should be stated, however, that these topics, when illustrated in their proper connections in the regular class-teaching, will not have the undue prominence that was given them designedly in this brief course of lessons.

The printed notes indicate the arrangement and method followed; but the lessons were not written out at the time they were given, and no attempt has been made to reproduce them in full.

Boston, April 7, 1883.

INTRODUCTORY.

THE inquiry *why* we teach geography naturally precedes the consideration of *how* we ought to teach it.

Let us assume that our main purpose is to give our pupils a real knowledge of the earth on which they live. This implies that we wish to lead them to perceive its wonderful adaptation to the wants of man; its resources for food, clothing, shelter, and for the arts and industries of civilized society. They should catch glimpses of its marvellous beauty and grandeur; and should find the close relations that exist between physical conditions and the life of different nations.

As teachers of geography we shall draw upon our largest resources in natural and physical science, in general history, and in art and literature. However elementary our instruction, we shall need a wide range of knowledge, as we travel, in imagination, with our pupils, over the broad earth; helping them to see phases of nature and of life, on sea and land, in hot and cold countries, on mountains and deserts, and among untutored and civilized people.

Geography, well taught, is an educational study, cultivating the imagination and judgment, as well as the memory; training the mind in both observation and language. Perhaps no other branch in the grammar-school curriculum gives opportunity for culture in so many directions. And there is no subject taught in which it is more necessary for the teacher to be independent of the text-book, especially in the arrangement of lessons, and in the apportionment of time, according to the relative importance of the parts of the subject.

Text-books of geography must give more names, statistics, and facts than we wish to keep in our minds, or to have our pupils learn. They are, in a sense, reference books; correct, for the time, in many statements that will be untrue before the children of to-day take our places. We should not, then, cumber their memories with what may prove worse than useless rubbish, because not so easily disposed of.

Are we, then, to discard text-books? Certainly not; but we are to make them our helpers, not our guides. Are we to dispense with memory-work for our pupils? Certainly not. We must have it, or our teaching will fail in results. But we must put life and color into the dry facts of our text-books, and give, for the memory-lessons, only intelligent summaries of the valuable points of the instruction.

Are we to require the study of map-questions? Assuredly; but not the learning of a catalogue of names. There has been no real addition to geographical knowledge, when pupils have learned to repeat names with which they have no other associations than the places they occupy upon the map.

Are we to have definitions accurately stated? Certainly; but only when the thing to be defined, and the language that expresses the definition, are clearly comprehended.

Are we to have question and answer, or topical recitations? Surely both have a place. During the presentation of new points the Socratic method is the true one. The teacher must excite mental activity in the class by skilful questioning. The children must be led to think, to examine, and to express the results of their study. The teacher should *tell them nothing they can naturally find out for themselves;* but their earnest study should be supplemented by bits of information, vivid descriptions, and other illustrations, given by the teacher, in their proper connection. This, and this alone, is *true oral instruction, the direction of the mental activity of the pupils.* After this come the memory-lessons, the definitions, and, finally, the reproducing of the different points of the geography of any country, by topical recitations. These should be the independent efforts of the pupils, expressed in their own language.

In the process of instruction a geographical vocabulary is formed. This should be fully grasped in both its spoken and its written forms. Hard words for children, perhaps we say. But do not children, like unlettered adults, seek the long words, and do they not insist upon having the right name for every new thing? They should have the habit of taking each new word through the eye, as well as the ear, and thus a geographical vocabulary, correct in spelling and pronunciation, will have a natural and gradual growth.

We come finally to the question of reviews. Should not the main points of the last lesson be gathered up before proceeding to the next in order? Is there not need of a careful review, whenever the instruction on any topic or subject is completed, before passing to the next? Are not the best reviews often given incidentally, whenever points of previous instruction are referred to? Is not the application of knowledge previously acquired always its surest test? In this way only do pupils appreciate the need of recovering lost knowledge. Let us have reviews, frequent and thorough, without dull repetition, by putting the old facts or inferences into new connections; and, by showing the need of information, give the incentive to acquire it. Let our pupils, while taking new steps, find their dependence upon steps previously taken.

It is of great importance to have the course of study continuous and progressive, though pupils may pursue it under the care of different teachers. Thus only can the best geographical results be secured in graded schools. Let us, then, so far as is possible in four hours, consider an outline for a course of study, and methods of carrying it out, in successive classes, in its three departments of physical, civil, and astronomical geography.

METHODS OF TEACHING GEOGRAPHY.

PREPARATION FOR THE STUDY OF GEOGRAPHY IN THE PRIMARY SCHOOLS.

IN some towns and cities the study of geography is begun in the primary schools. Whether or not this is the case, the preparation for it should be made there, and the success and interest of the early lessons in geography depend largely upon the previous training of the pupils.

A progressive course of observation lessons, running through the primary classes, will naturally include lessons on color, form, place, plants, animals, the sky, clouds, rain, snow, the natural features of the vicinity, etc. The relation of these to the study of geography is evident. A familiar knowledge of their surroundings will make children eager to know about other parts of the earth; ready to see them through the imagination, so vivid in childhood. Color and form are elements in the appreciation of the simplest descriptions. Maps will be needed to put distant places in their relative positions; but maps are misleading unless children are prepared for their use by simple, illustrated lessons on place, direction, and distance. A teacher, about to give the first lessons in geography, should discover whether or not the class has received proper preparatory training. If not, such lessons as are here indicated should be given as an indispensable preparation.

I. Lessons on Place (including Relative Position, Direction, and Distance).

1. (*a*) Illustrations of the use of the prepositions of place; as *on, above, before, between, under, below, behind, around,* etc.

METHOD.
By placing objects.

The teacher places . . . . the pupil imitates.
The teacher places . . . . the pupil describes.
The teacher dictates . . . . the pupil places.
The teacher disarranges . . the pupil replaces from memory.

(*b*) Illustrations of the use of the terms right, left, middle, centre, corner, etc.

Lessons as above.

Right-hand corner ⎫
Left-hand corner ⎪
Front right-hand corner ⎬ of table or desk.
Back left-hand corner ⎪
Middle of right side, etc., ⎭

(*c*) Representations by the pupils of the relative position of objects.

By drawing on their slates the form of desk or table, and marking the position of objects on it.

2. (*a*) The necessity for a *standard of distance* shown.

Near to . . . . far from.
Nearer to . . . . farther from.
How near ? . . . . how far away ?
A long way off . . . . how far ?

(b) Measurements in the school-room: either in inches, feet, yards; or in metres, decimetres, centimetres.

(c) Representations on a scale, of the top of a desk or table, and of the floor, with the places of a few objects designated.

Thus far Primary-School work, and these lessons lead directly to the preparation for the use of maps.

II. Lessons on Plants and Animals.

That live on the *land;* in the *water;* in the *air.*

That have their home in *hot parts* of the earth; in *cold parts;* in *forests;* in *plains* and *deserts;* on *mountains.*

Most of the children have eaten the fruits of warm climates. They have seen the animals that usually belong to a menagerie or circus, and know that many of them are brought across the great *ocean* from other lands.

III. Stories and reading-lessons about people who live far away.

In what kind of homes?   What they eat?
What they wear?   What they do?
What animals they use?

The friends of many of the children have been far away over *sea* or *land.* What have the children heard of their journeys?

IV. General knowledge gained by most children before beginning the study of geography.

1. Of *land* and *water.*

Of the uses of each (for living, travelling, food-products, etc.).

Of different modes of travelling (transportation).

Of different occupations of people (familiar and unfamiliar).
Of different people and their ways of living (manners and customs).
Of different natural features (hill, pond, and island).

2. Of *air* all around, over land and water (atmosphere).
Of a draught of air (wind).
Of the quick drying of mud, clothes, etc., in a warm air; in a windy day.
Of the different forms of water (fog, clouds, rain, snow, hail).

3. Of the sun as giving light and heat.
Of the sun, moon, and stars, as far away.
Of divisions of time: — day, night; week, month, year; spring, summer, autumn, winter.

4. Of the terms circle, circumference, diameter, sphere, hemisphere (from the lessons in drawing and form.)

BEGINNINGS IN GEOGRAPHY,

Or, A FIRST COURSE OF LESSONS.

A PLAN OF WORK, BASED ON THE PRELIMINARY KNOWLEDGE GAINED IN THE PRIMARY SCHOOLS.

As the children have already a notion of land and water; of people living far away; of hot climates where oranges and bananas grow, and where lions and tigers live; and of cold climates where the fur-bearing animals are found; it seems desirable to lead them at once to think of geography as the study by which they are to learn about the great world on which they live, and over which people travel either for business or pleasure.

A few introductory lessons, that appeal to the imagination of the children, and excite interest by calling out whatever knowledge they may have, will present to them the idea of the whole earth, before taking up the study of topography, which should, of course, begin with the immediate surroundings; taking first whatever natural features are best known, and leading out to the study of the various forms of land and water.

These first lessons should be entirely oral, the teacher using a vivid style and familiar language. The children should be encouraged to tell what they know already. The aim should be to create an interest in the different natural features and productions of the earth; and to describe simply the habits and occupations of people of distant lands, — thus giving a human interest to geography. The treatment of the subjects cannot be too simple or familiar.

The geographical vocabulary, spoken and written, should be formed as new words are introduced.

I. **Lessons to lead children to a simple conception of the earth as a great ball**
        moving in the air,
        lighted by the sun,
        with a surface of land and water.

(Address their imaginations, making "word-pictures").

Illustrations: — A ball tossed into the air. — A balloon in the air. — Birds in the air everywhere. — Boys in other places flying kites. — Air all over the round earth. — A picture of a globe floating in air.

The evening star, another earth.
The moon, a small earth.

Illustrations of shape. — Beads, marbles, balls, oranges, and the globe, shown *for form only*, not for shapes of land and water until preparation for the use of maps has been made. — Alike in shape, — different in size.

Illustration of the flat appearance. — A piece of cardboard, with a small, round hole in the middle, placed on a large globe.

Illustration of size. — Imagine a horse-car track laid around the earth, — more than half a year, day and night included, required for a single passage.

Illustration of the two motions. — Let one pupil stand for the sun; another pupil carry the globe round him, rotating it all the time.

Results of the two motions. — Day and night. A year. (Sufficient knowledge for this stage of the study).

Axis — Real and imaginary.
Poles of the axis.
Circumference — diameter.
Equator, as related to poles.
(Illustrations — A ball and a knitting-needle — A spinning-top.

Hot parts, as related to equator.
Cold parts, as related to poles.
Temperate parts, as between hot and cold parts.
Climate, as name for kind of weather.

II. Lessons on the natural features of the surface.

Begin with the most familiar. — A hill, a pond, a stream, a coast-line, islands, whatever can be seen by the class. "1. Observe. 2. Name. 3. Describe."

Aids to teaching. — Pictures; blackboard illustrations; moulding-board. "Our World" No. 1, by Miss Hall.

As a new feature is introduced, ascertain whether any child has seen or heard of it. If a feature, an island, for instance, cannot be observed, make a sketch on the blackboard or show a picture (not a map). Let the children note that it is approached by a boat or ship. Show another picture with a peninsula, and call for the difference between an island and a peninsula. A class is thus prepared for a concise statement, for a definition of a natural feature.

A large wooden tray and a few quarts of moulders' sand, with which the children may represent mountains, valleys, a coast-line, islands, etc., will be very serviceable. By this means children, from the start, associate relief as well as horizontal forms with the land-surface. The land is treated as a solid, having length, breadth, and height. The moulding-board will show differences in level on a sea coast; the distinction between cape and promontory; the gradual rise of the land from the sea-level to a mountain system; the valleys for rivers, and why they run in all directions; the mountain slopes, and how minerals are accessible. With a piece of mica or glass to represent the sea-level, the varied character of the sea-bottom, with submarine mountains, border islands, the foundations for coral reefs, etc., may be indicated. The first outlines may be drawn from moulded forms, before maps are introduced.

The objection that reliefs are greatly exaggerated seems of little weight in comparison with the many advantages of a moulding-board. Exaggerated illustrations are often allowable in order to produce strong impressions. Indeed, we seldom think of forms of relief as they really are, in comparison with the whole surface of the earth; but we consider them as they appear to the eye, in comparison with the small visible portion of the surface, and their physical influences, which cannot be over-estimated.

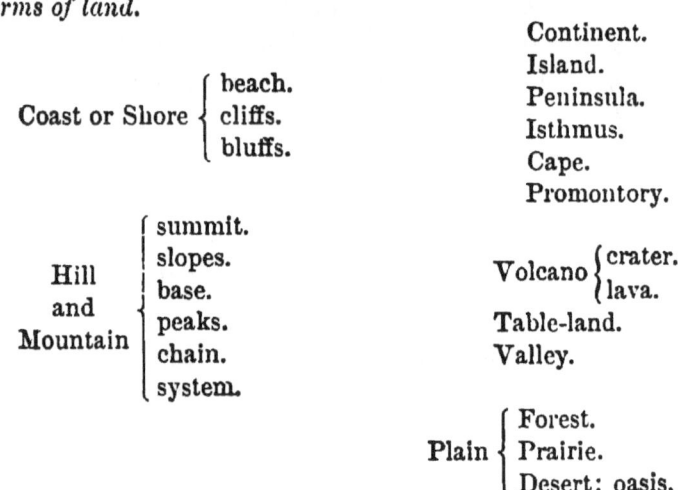

Forms of land.

Coast or Shore { beach. cliffs. bluffs. }

Hill and Mountain { summit. slopes. base. peaks. chain. system. }

Continent.
Island.
Peninsula.
Isthmus.
Cape.
Promontory.

Volcano { crater. lava. }
Table-land.
Valley.

Plain { Forest. Prairie. Desert: oasis. }

The water.
{ The great salt ocean flowing around and between the continents.
Fresh water flowing through the land. }

Forms of water.
Springs, — Brooks, — Rivers, — Lakes, — How formed?

{ Pure water. Mineral. Hot. Geysers. }

{ Branches. Source. Current. Mouth. Banks. Waterfalls. Uses. }

Sea, — Gulf, — Bay, — Harbor, — Strait, — Channel, — Sound.

METHODS OF TEACHING GEOGRAPHY. 17

III. **Lessons in connection with the study of the natural features.**
   Principal occupations of the people of the earth included in these lessons.

   What the earth affords *on* its land-surface.

   Vegetation.
   For food and drink (agriculture).

   For clothing (manufactures).

   For fuel.
   For medicine.
   For building-material (lumbering).
   For oils and dyes.
   For utensils.

   Animals.
   For food { live-stock. dairy-products.

   For clothing { furs. skins. leather.

   For labor.
   For utensils { ivory. bone.

   Some specially useful plants.
   Cotton-plant.   Palms.
   Sugar-cane.   Bamboo.
   Rice.   Coffee-plant.
   Grape-vine.   Tea-plant.
   Fruits of our climate.
   Fruits of hot climates.

   Specially useful animals.
   Horse.   Dog.
   Cow.   Sheep.
   Reindeer.   Goat.
   Camel.   Silkworm.

   What the earth affords *under* its land-surface: —
   Building stones (quarrying).
   Metals, ⎫
   Coal,   ⎬ mining — manufactures.
   Salt.   ⎭

   What the water affords: —
   Fish (fisheries).   Sea-weed.
   Shell-fish.   Salt.
   Whales (whale-ships, oil,   Pearls.
     whalebone).   Coral (reefs — islands).
   Sponge.

The Atmosphere.
Air necessary to life — (illustrations).
Air in motion — (wind).
Moisture in the air — visible — invisible — evaporated — condensed, — (familiar illustrations).

IV. Introduction of Maps.
1. (*a*) Review primary-school lessons on Position, Distance, Direction. (See pp. 10, 11).

   (*b*). Show the necessity for a *standard of direction*.
   1. Tell a pupil to walk to the right, then *turn* and walk to the right. (Thus show that he may walk to the right and reach opposite points of the room).
   2. Pass from the relative terms, right, left, etc., to the absolute terms, north, south, east, west.
      Children facing the sun at noon — look south. Their shadows — fall north. (True for any place north of the Tropic of Cancer).
      Facing the sunset — look toward the west.
      Facing the sunrise — look toward the east.

   (*c*) Show compass. Mark lines of direction on the floor. Give practical exercises to teach N., E., S., W., N.E., S.E., N.W., S.W.
   Children walk, point, tell the direction of objects.
   Children find the directions of other class-rooms; of other places from the school-house.
   Tell how to go to their homes; give the directions.

   (*d*) Let the children represent on slates the table-top, floor, etc., keeping points of compass.
   Do not confuse the children by making representations at first on the upright blackboard. When they are familiar with a plan drawn on their slates, let them hold their slates upright, with the north at the top.

METHODS OF TEACHING GEOGRAPHY.

(e) Let them study a good plan (map) of the immediate vicinity.

It will be convenient to draw it on a sheet of blackboard paper, which may be placed horizontally at first, and afterward in an upright position.
Take imaginary walks on it. Note directions taken. Settle doubts by actual observation.

2. (a) Study a map of the city or town, or of a part of it.
  A stranger would like such a map — why?
  Show where the surrounding towns are.
  Find natural features, hill, pond, stream, etc.
  Find direction of principal streets.
  Describe places of interest.

  (b) Let the children find the scale of the map; determine distances upon it.

3. (a) Show the need of maps. How the early travellers made maps. Difference between picture and map.

  (b) Let the children draw from the moulded form a representation of coast-line, with bay, cape, peninsula, island, etc.

  (c) Show an outline map of a continent (one without names preferable).
  Let the children learn to read the map-symbols for mountains, rivers, etc.

  (d) Let the children find the natural features on maps of other continents or grand divisions.

  (e) Find corresponding maps in the geographies.
  Compare scales. Compare scales of maps of the grand divisions.

(*f*) Find corresponding maps on the globe; find relative position and size.

(*g*) Pass from the globe to the maps of hemispheres. (Each map represents half the surface of a globe on a flat surface; illustrate).

V. General study of the Maps of Hemispheres:—

The Continents or Grand Divisions.
　Their names — number — *relative* position and size.

The Oceans.
　Pacific — largest, many islands { volcanic, coral.
　Atlantic — best known, most travelled, many gulfs and bays.
　Indian — warm, small { pearls, spices, coral, sponge.
　Arctic and Antarctic { cold, icebergs, whales, seals, sea-fowl.

Important Islands.
　East Indies — hot climate { coffee, spices, gums.
　West Indies — hot climate { fruits, salt, cigars, sugar.
　Iceland — volcano, geysers.
　Sandwich Islands — warm climate, much trade, in mid-ocean.
　Azores — fine climate, in mid-ocean.
　British Islands — (with Europe).
　Japan Islands — (with Asia).
　Newfoundland — (with North America).

METHODS OF TEACHING GEOGRAPHY. 21

VI. General Study of the Grand Divisions.

Children like the strange and wonderful, are interested in the people and products of other lands; therefore it is well to take early the striking differences in nature and in the people of the earth, before beginning the study of the countries of the grand divisions in order.

"The Seven Little Sisters," and the companion volume "Each and All," by Miss Andrews; "Aunt Martha's Corner Cupboard, or Stories about Tea, Coffee, Sugar, etc.," by M. and E. Kirby; and "Little Lucy's Wonderful Globe," by Miss Yonge; will furnish collateral reading.

Pictures, blackboard illustrations, vivid descriptions, specimens of products, etc., will be of great service.

Map-drawing, as an aid in fixing in the memory the forms of the grand divisions, the position of mountain-systems, and of the chief rivers, lakes, and cities, should be begun early. Children should not be expected, however, to draw correct outlines at first; and it is unwise to let them even see incorrect ones, therefore they should be allowed to trace them, for a time. Teachers may secure good beginnings in map-drawing by preparing cardboard forms of the grand divisions, corresponding in size with the maps in the text-book. When a grand division is studied, let each pupil have one of these cardboard forms (several of a kind may be needed for use in a large class) long enough to mark round it upon slate or paper. With an accurate outline thus drawn, it will be easy for the children to copy, from their maps, the mountains, rivers, and cities selected for study. The close attention required for this hand-work will help to fix forms and relative positions in the memory.

22 METHODS OF TEACHING GEOGRAPHY.

Outline for the Study of the Grand Divisions.

Position on the globe.
 Climate — where hot, cold, temperate?
Relative Position and Size.
 Refer to globe and maps of hemispheres.
Surrounding Oceans.

Interesting facts and associations.
{
Form and Outline (character of coast).
 Chief projections and indentations.
 Study of outline by tracing or drawing, not from memory.
Mountain-Systems.
 Comparative Height.
 Direction of Slopes (Drainage).
 Plateaus — Valleys — Plains.
 Indicate mountains on the outline map.
Rivers and Lakes (principal ones only).
 Source — Mouth, or outlet.
 Relative Length.
 Indicate rivers and lakes on the outline maps.
Most valuable Productions — where?
The important Countries and their People.
A few well-known Cities.
Specially interesting localities.
}

Special points for North America.

Greenland (for a cold country) {
 Esquimaux.
 Story of "Agoonack," one of "The Seven Little Sisters."
}

British America. — Forests, furs, hunters, trappers.

United States. — Our country {
 Middle part,
 Temperate climate,
 Many productions.
}

Mexico. — Hot, unhealthful coast-line — high, pleasant table-lands — cattle-raising, prickly pear, cochineal.

For South America.

Hot, forest lands, trees, animals, products, story of "The Little Brown Baby."

Grassy plains, cattle — Andes region, mines, earthquakes, volcanoes — Patagonia, dreary country, savages.

METHODS OF TEACHING GEOGRAPHY. 23

For Europe.
> Many civilized nations.
> Many occupations.
> Many colonies sent to many parts of the world.
> Mountain and river scenery.
> Climate and products of different parts.
> Interesting cities.
> Stories of "The Little Mountain Maiden" and of "The Child of the beautiful River Rhine."
> Story of "The Little Merchants," by Miss Edgeworth, for Vesuvius.

For Asia.
> The largest grand division — all climates.
> Highest mountains.
> Siberia — cold, furs, forests, rivers.
> Palestine, or Holy Land.
> Arabs, Chinese, Japanese, Hindoos.
> Special animals and vegetation.
> Story of "Pen-Se."
> "Little People of Asia," by Olive Thorne Miller.

For Africa.
> The least civilized of the grand divisions.
> Climate mostly hot — Sahara, caravans.
> Nile — overflow, pyramids.
> Negro tribes. Lion, elephant, giraffe, etc. Palms, indigo, etc.
> Stories of "Gemila" and "Manenko."

For Australia.
> Hot climate, droughts.
> Gold, wool, queer animals and plants.

Summary of the Study of the Grand Divisions.

Example. To be made by the Children.

Grand Division.	Size, relative.	Position.	Climate.	Mountains.	Rivers and Lakes.	PRODUCTIONS.			People.
						Mineral.	Vegetable.	Animal.	
ASIA.	Largest.	Old World, Northern Hemisphere.	All climates. Very hot. Very cold.	Highest. Run from E. to W. Himalaya, Altai, Ural.	Ganges, Indus, Euphrates, Yang tse Kiang, Hoang Ho, Yenesei. Not many lakes.	Gold, Silver, Iron, Precious Stones.	Rice, Cotton, Indigo, Bamboo, Tea, Coffee, Jungles, Pine forests.	Tiger, Elephant, Serpents, Camel, Silk-worm, Goat, Fur-bearing.	Chinese. Japanese. Arabs. Hindoos. Turks. English. Russians.
AFRICA.	Second.	Old World, Northern and Southern Hemispheres.	Mostly hot. Crossed by the Equator.	Atlas, Kong, Snow.	Nile, Niger, Zambesi, Orange. Many large lakes. Albert, Victoria, Tchad.	Gold, Gold-dust, Diamonds.	Palms, Cotton, Indigo, Gum-trees, Bulbs, Grains.	Lion, Elephant (*ivory*), Camel, Hippopotamus, Rhinoceros, Crocodile, Gorilla, Apes, Hyena, Ostrich, Giraffe, Sheep (*wool*).	Arabs. Turks. Egyptians. Negroes. Dutch. English.

Tabulate one grand division at a time. Children tell. Teacher write on the blackboard. Then each pupil write from memory.
In review.—Tabulate all the grand divisions. Compare. Trace similarities and differences.

METHODS OF TEACHING GEOGRAPHY. 25

VII. Method of Study for the Countries of a Grand Division.

The children are now prepared to take up such study of *the countries* of each grand division as is adapted to their age.

"Scribner's Geographical Reader" (based upon "Guyot's Introduction"), and "Our World," No. I., will be useful for collateral reading. Books of travel, etc., for special countries, will add to the interest of the lessons.

Map-drawing, as an accompaniment to the study of a country, will prove an important aid. Let the reproduction of an outline help the study of the outline; the placing of mountains, etc., be a means of learning their position. Pupils should not, however, be burdened with much memory-drawing, nor distracted by drawing the map of one country and studying another. Practice on the map of a country already studied may, however, at any time be useful as a review; and when, later in the course, certain maps are to be held in the memory, occasional practice will be desirable.

Example. — A plan for the study of New England.
Preparation implied.
    America — the New World — how discovered?
    West Indies — why so called?
    First settlements in South and North America.
    (First chapters in "Stories of American History," by N. S. Dodge, and selections from other books, as collateral reading.)
    Appearance of our country when discovered.
    Indians — European colonies.
    The United States — how formed?
    The thirteen original States — where?
    Present extent of the United States.
    General study of the United States.
    New England — in what part of the United States.
    What mountain-system crosses it?

1. Have a map of New England.

   Have the moulded form, showing direction of mountain-ranges and slopes, drainage, rivers, and lakes.

   Why called New England?
   Names of the six States.
   Coast-line, articulation of.
   Other Boundaries.
   Mountains.
       Two main ranges — highest peak, summits, slopes, trees, scenery, rock quarries — "Granite State."
   Drainage.
       Valleys, Rivers (rapid currents useful for?), Lakes.
   Climate.
   Different kinds of Surface.

   Different Occupations of the people { quarrying, lumbering, fishing, commerce, manufactures, farming.

   Where the good places for Cities?
   Find the most important cities noted for { manufactures, commerce and trade, capitals.
   Description of interesting localities, cities, etc.

2. Combine map-drawing with study.

   The children are now prepared for such study of the text-book as is desirable. Ready to seek information elsewhere. Pictures, specimens, etc., as aids. Map-drawing as the study proceeds.

   (*Put no names on the map at first. Memory-drawing not required.*)

   (*a*) Review study of outline.
       Draw the outline (on paper).
       Draw boundaries between the States.

   (*b*) Review mountains.
       Indicate mountains on the outline map.

(c) Review rivers and lakes.
: Indicate rivers and lakes on the map.

(d) Review cities.
: Indicate cities on the map.

(e) Make a general review.
: Put on the map, from memory, names of bays, capes, islands, mountain-ranges, rivers, lakes, and cities.

3. Let the children give a summary of the knowledge gained, without questions, in the order of topics.
Describe imaginary journeys.
Write letters from different places.

More or less time should be given to the sections of our own country, and to the other countries of the world, according to their relative importance.

A few striking points, strongly made, would be sufficient for the whole continent of Africa, in this first course.

Example.

1. — **Africa.**
Thorough training with the use of maps as to the *position* of Africa and its relation to other grand divisions. Regular *coast-line*, disadvantages of. *Mountains* — Chains along the coast, the highest on the east, Atlas, Kong, Snow mountains. *Rivers* — Nile, flowing northward; Congo, Niger, Zambesi, and other rivers flowing into the Atlantic and Indian oceans. *Divisions* — Egypt, Abyssinia, Barbary States, Sahara, Soudan, Guinea, Cape Colony. *Cities* — Cairo, Alexandria, Suez, Algiers, Cape Town.

2. — North Africa.

Atlas Mountains along the northern coast; hilly country on the borders of the torrid zone. Climate pleasant, nearly tropical. Date and gum trees, fragrant and medicinal plants. Lions, gazelles, hyenas, jackals. Exports — dates, nuts, oil, sponge.

People not negroes, but Arabs, Moors, Turks — all Mohammedans. Some civilized, living in cities; others wandering Arabs, living in tents.

Dress and customs of Mohammedans. Characteristics of Mohammedan cities — narrow streets, flat house-tops, mosques, etc. (Selections from Lane's "Modern Egyptians"; Bayard Taylor's "Lands of the Saracen.")

Egypt — a narrow valley between the desert and the Red Sea. Suez canal. The Nile, its course, overflow, delta. Cultivation of cotton, wheat, sugar-cane, etc. — Villages and palm trees along the river; no forests; pyramids and ruins along its lower course, (mention of ancient history); cities near the mouth. — (See "Egypt," by Stanley Lane-Poole; "Egypt and Nubia," by J. A. St. John.)

3. — Sahara.

The great desert — sandy levels, rocky ridges, oases, sand-storms; Bedouins; caravans coming and going between northern cities and towns of Soudan; stories and pictures of desert life.

4. — Almost Unexplored Region.

Great wilderness inhabited by uncivilized negro tribes, wearing little clothing, living in circular mud huts with thatched roofs, using rough earthenware, mats, etc; occupation chiefly hunting and warfare. Some of the more advanced tribes make cotton cloth in small pieces, spears, anklets of iron and copper, and cultivate patches of cotton, indigo, and millet. Manners and customs. Rivers with crocodiles and hippopotami. In the forests, elephants, lions, antelopes, giraffes, gorillas, apes, etc. — (See the works of Livingstone, Stanley, and other explorers.)

5. — **West and East Coasts.**

Low, hot, tropical country; rice, peanuts, castor-oil plant, and thick forests or jungle along the rivers. Native huts, and here and there small trading towns (Portuguese and English), where merchants exchange calico, guns, knives, beads, etc., for ivory, ostrich-feathers, and beeswax, which the natives bring from the interior; and for palm-oil, peanuts, rice, gold-dust, etc., obtained on the coast.

6. — **Cape Colony.**

In possession of the English. Story of the discovery of the Cape. Country hilly, with mountain-ranges from east to west. Pleasant, temperate climate. Grain, bulbs, wine. Dutch sheep-farmers inland. Ostrich-farming. Gold and diamond diggings. Cape Town. Wool the chief export.

7. — **Islands.**

Madagascar, one of the largest islands on the globe. High mountains. Peculiar plants and animals. St. Helena, a rocky island, in mid-ocean. Place of Napoleon's exile. Cape Verd, Canary, and Madeira Islands; volcanic; pleasant climate; vineyards; canary-birds.

Note. — For other books on Africa, see list on pp. 69-71.

A SECOND COURSE OF LESSONS.

A first course, for children, should be mainly observational and descriptive, with only such inferences in regard to physical influences as the children can be led to make from facts observed by them or given to them. If this course creates an interest in the further study of the world, and gives, to those pupils who may not take a second course, a knowledge of the different natural features and products, and of the life of people in the different parts of the earth, the desired ends are accomplished.

A second course should be more logical and systematic though, in both statements and illustrations, it should still be simple.

As the climate of any part of the earth depends primarily on its solar heat, and as natural products and civilization depend mainly upon climate, it is important that this second course should be based upon the consideration of the earth's relations to the sun.

I. The Form of the Earth.

The ancient nations, living around the Mediterranean, believed that the earth was a great, circular plain, surrounded by an ocean, from which the sun rose, and into which it set. The earliest descriptions and maps of the world that have been preserved (about 500 B.C.) tell us this.

Long before the time of Columbus, learned men believed the form of the earth to be that of a globe; but the belief was not general.

Columbus thought he had reached India, when he found America; and this fact shows that he had no conception of the *size* of the earth.

Proofs of its Form.

(a) Magellan's Voyage (1520).
(b) Vessels coming in sight —
    Vessels going out of sight — how seen?
    Illustration — a toy ship on a globe.
    Cause — curvature of the surface of the sea.
(c) Sailors approaching land — what first seen?
(d) Horizon — the *circle* of vision.
    Everywhere a circle.
    Horizon on a plain.
    Ascending a hill.
(e) Shadow of the earth — eclipse of the moon.
    Only a sphere can always cast a circular shadow. Illustrate.

True Form.

Spheroidal, not spherical.   Difference in diameters.

II. Size of the Earth.

Circumference at the equator.
Diameter at the equator.
Diameter in direction of the axis.
Illustration. — Time for railroad train to go round the circumference (25,000 miles). — Rate, 30 miles an hour. — More than a month, making no stops.

III. Latitude and Longitude.

Means of fixing the position of places on the earth necessary. Illustrate.

Lessons with the use of a globe.

Find Equator — where? It is the circumference of a circle — where the centre of the circle? — where the plane of the circle? (Accustom the pupils to the planes of circles before teaching the plane of the orbit. Cut apples to illustrate.)
The Equator a *great* circle.
Find Parallels — why not great circles?
        centres where?
        planes where?

Every circumference divided into 360 degrees.
" " measures four right angles.
The length of degrees differs on the parallels.
Parallels mark distances north and south of the Equator — called Latitude.
What else needed to fix the position of a place?
No natural starting-place (or circle) from which to reckon distance east and west.
Different countries use different circles.
They must be north and south circles.
They must all pass through the poles.
They mark the line of the mid-day shadow at any place — the *north* and *south line*.
They are therefore called Meridians (from mid-day).
Every place has such a line for mid-day shadows.
Extended, it makes a circle passing through the poles.
On the semicircle opposite the place is the midnight line — or the mid-day line for the place opposite.
All the meridians are great circles —
having their centres where?
having their planes where?
How find the direction of the meridian of a place on a sunny day?
How find the direction of the meridian on a starry night?
How can a sailor or traveller find the direction of the meridian of a place at any time?
Where would a person standing on the north pole see the pole-star?
Where, if standing on the equator?
Where do we see the pole-star?
How find the north and south points of the horizon from the pole-star?
Draw a vertical semicircle in the air to connect the north and south points of the horizon?
It will pass through the *zenith*.
Observatories have such a visible north and south semicircle, very carefully placed. Therefore such a circle is taken to reckon east and west distances from.
One at Greenwich, England;
" Paris, France;
" Washington.
We reckon generally from the English starting-point.

East and West distances, called Longitude. 180° East; 180° West.

North and South distances, called Latitude. 90° North; 90° South.

Why these terms used ? (They would not be selected now.)

All places on the meridian of Greenwich have no Longitude, when that meridian is used as the *First* or *Prime* Meridian.

Give the class practice in finding the Latitude and Longitude of certain places, and in finding places when Latitude and Longitude are given.

Latitude, measured where ?

Longitude, measured where ?

Why degrees of Longitude vary in length ? (Pupils discover.)

Sailors, on the ocean, can find their Latitude and Longitude (the place of their ship) by observing the sun.

IV. The Motions of the Earth — Effects.

1. The round earth floats in space, as a balloon floats in the air.

    It is lighted by the sun. How?

    Illustration. — Hold a ball in the sunlight or before a lighted lamp.

    However it is held, *one half* is lighted.

    The same is true of the earth.

    1st point. — Always a hemisphere lighted.

    If the ball and light are both motionless, the same hemisphere is always lighted.

    What effects, if this were true of the earth ?

    Turn the ball on its axis once. (Knitting-needle for axis.)

    2d point. — Observe the lighted hemisphere constantly changing.

    Why ?

2. Rotation.

    Then the turning of our earth on its axis gives us day and night.

    Evidences of the earth's rotation.

Apparent daily movement of the heavenly bodies.

Illustration. { In a moving railway car.
{ Real and apparent motion.

The *difference in the speed* of rotation of different parts.
Greatest speed at the equator — about 1,000 miles an hour.
Speed decreasing toward the poles.

(*a*) Let the axis of the ball (representing the earth) be upright.

    Rotate and observe effect.
    Let a pupil put on a cardboard disc, or day circle, to separate the light and dark hemispheres.
    It passes over the poles.
    Day and night everywhere alternately.

(*b*) Let the axis be horizontal. Rotate.

    The day circle will correspond with the equator.
    The same hemisphere always lighted.

(*c*) Let the axis be oblique. Rotate.

    The day circle neither passes over the poles nor corresponds with the equator.
    Around one pole, constant day.
    Around the other pole, constant night.
    Is any one of the three cases (*a*, *b*, *c*) true for our Earth?
    Then there is something more to find out; but we will first illustrate sunrise — noon — sunset — midnight — for some place.
    Use the day circle or a black cap covering a hemisphere ("night cap"), and a wafer, on a ball or globe.
    We say the sun rises at any place when that place turns into the sun's light. (Real and apparent motion.)
    Give practice in finding sunrise, etc., for different places on the ball.
    Have you observed whether or not the sun rises and sets at the same time through the year?
    Is the sun ever higher or lower in the sky, when you go from school at noon, than it is now?
    Let us find out the reason for these differences.

METHODS OF TEACHING GEOGRAPHY. 35

3. Revolution. Changes of Seasons.
- (*a*) Who can tell about another movement of our earth?

    We will give our ball the other movement. What are the names of the two poles of the earth's axis?
    If I call the upper end of the ball's axis the *north* pole, how shall I hold the ball?
    Place the ball with its axis pointed rightly and inclined rightly, and with the north pole turned toward the light. Let a pupil put on a disc or cap, as before.
    How is the earth lighted now?
    Which pole is in sunshine?
    Can any one tell which of our seasons this represents?

- (*b*) Carry the ball to the opposite side of the lamp (thus making a strong contrast in conditions).

    Let a pupil arrange disc or cap now.
    How is the earth lighted now?
    Which of our seasons is represented? Why?

- (*c*) Carry the globe through the next quarter-revolution.

    Let a pupil arrange now for the lighted hemisphere.
    Tell how the earth is lighted now?
    Which of our seasons now? Why?

- (*d*) Complete the revolution. Restore and describe the first conditions (given under *a*). Pass through the next quarter-revolution.

    Describe conditions for our spring and for autumn in the other hemisphere.

- (*e*) Give sufficient practice to strengthen the points made.

    Let a pupil take the ball, arrange it, and make the revolution. Class observe — tell the seasons. Finally have written descriptions.

Summary.
> Then the changes of the seasons are caused by (1) the revolution of the earth around the sun; (2) the inclination of the earth's axis; and (3) the unvarying direction of the axis. Any two of these causes, acting without the third, would not produce a change of seasons.
>> Let pupils illustrate the action of two conditions without the third.

4. Variation in the Length of Day and Night.
   (*a*) Introducing both motions of the ball.
   > Draw the equator and the parallel of the city or town where the school is.
   > Pupils find which circle is exactly half-lighted, however the disc is put on.
   > What about the lighting of the parallel?
   > Mark the place for their city or town with a wafer.

   (*b*) Put the ball in position for the northern midsummer.
   > Put the wafer in position for sunrise.
   > Show where on the same parallel it is sunset.
   > Mark this place with another wafer.
   > Rotate the ball.
   > Are these wafers longer in the dark or in the light?
   > What do you know then about day and night, on our parallel, at this time of the year?

   (*c*) With the ball in the same position, put a wafer on the part of the earth where Agoonack, the Esquimaux girl, lives (see p. 22).
   > Tell about her day and season.
   > Hold a crayon on the farthest point of the surface beyond the north pole that sunlight reaches.
   > Rotate. — Keep the crayon in position and let it draw a circle as the ball rotates.
   > Rotate again. — Pupils watch and tell about the *day* of all places *within this circle*.

METHODS OF TEACHING GEOGRAPHY. 37

(*d*) Hold a crayon on the *central point* of the lighted hemisphere.

> Rotate. — Let the crayon draw a circle.
> Lead pupils to tell that *all places on this circle* have a *vertical sun* at noon.
> Rotate several times. — Pupils tell about the relative length of day and night in different places.

(*e*) Carry the earth through half a revolution.

> Pupils tell the conditions and seasons. Repeat the experiments and draw the corresponding circles for the southern hemisphere.
> Practice and reviews necessary.

(*f*) Where did we draw the polar circles?

Where did we draw the other two parallels?

Let us see upon what their places on the globe depend.

> Change the inclination of the axis.
> Rotate. — Pupils see that the places of these circles are changed.
> Then their places depend upon the slanting of the axis, — $23\frac{1}{2}$ degrees from the upright position.
> Remember that the axis inclines $23\frac{1}{2}$ degrees, and that each pole points always in the same direction.
> Practice and reviews needed.

(*g*) Place the ball in the intermediate positions for spring and autumn.

> Use day circle or cap as before.
> Lead pupils to see that *one half of each parallel* is lighted.
> Rotate. — Lead pupils to infer that days and nights are equal everywhere. (Say nothing of the poles).
> What season in each hemisphere?

(*h*) Carry the ball through a quarter-revolution slowly, rotating it all the time.

> Pupils notice and describe the *gradual* changes in season and length of day for either hemisphere. Give practice and reviews.

5. Tropics and Polar circles.

The pupils should be ready now to state —

(1) That the tropics mark the limits of a vertical sun. Why called *tropics?*
(2) That the polar circles mark the limits of the continuance of daylight for more than twenty-four hours.

> Lead the pupils to discover that the sun is overhead at the tropics, once each year.
> Overhead between the tropics, twice each year.
>   " at the northern tropic at our midsummer.
>   " " " southern tropic at our midwinter.
>   " " " equator in spring and autumn.
>   " at all places between equator and tropics at intermediate times.

6. Orbit and Plane of Orbit.

> Place a large, circular piece of cardboard around a globe or ball representing the sun.
> Hold a smaller ball (representing the earth) so that a hemisphere shall be above the cardboard (keeping conditions of axis).
> Lead pupils to see that the centres of the two balls are in the *plane* of the cardboard, and that this plane might surround the earth as it does the sun, and extend far in all directions.
> Lead them to imagine an *immense* distance between the balls; so that the space between the sun (the large ball) and the wall of the room behind it would be as nothing to any one on the earth (the small ball) looking at the sun. The sun would seem to such an observer to touch the

METHODS OF TEACHING GEOGRAPHY. 39

wall, as a tree on the top of a distant hill seems to touch the sky behind it.

Our sky seems like the inner surface of a hollow hemisphere (where is the other hemisphere?), with the sun, moon, and stars moving over it. So the sun seems to us to be among the stars. The stars are really *very much farther away than the sun*. If the school-room were dome-shaped, we might imagine its walls to be the sky for our balls. Let us try to do so.

Let the earth revolve round the edge of the cardboard (keeping conditions of axis, etc.).

Pupils (imagining the great distance) tell where, on the walls, the sun might seem to be, as seen from the revolving earth. (Perhaps near certain pictures on the walls, taken as stars.)

The path in which the earth moves round the sun is called *its orbit*.

The cardboard represents an imaginary *flat surface*, passing through the centres of both sun and earth, on which this path or orbit lies. This imaginary surface is called *the plane of the orbit*. { Imaginary axis. Imaginary plane.

Then the sun seems to move among the stars in the sky, because the earth really moves among them.

As the pictures on the walls have names, so groups of stars have names. Long ago people thought they could find pictures in the stars. One group was called a great bear, or a great dipper (who ever heard of that in the sky?); another a dog; another a warrior with his belt and sword (did any one ever see Orion on a beautiful winter night?), etc.

One of these groups of stars was called Cancer (a crab); and, as the sun seemed then to be in this group of stars when overhead to people on the northern tropic, we have the name *Tropic of Cancer*. (No attempt need be made to show the present distinction between constellations and signs of the zodiac.)

When the sun was overhead to people on the southern tropic, he seemed then to be among the stars that form the group called Capricornus (the goat); and so we have the name *Tropic of Capricorn*.

The north pole of the earth points to a group of stars called Arctos (the bear), and so we have the name *Arctic Circle.*

The opposite pole is named Anti (or opposite the) Arctic; and so we have the name *Antarctic Circle.*

- Tropical has come to mean hot, and Arctic to mean cold or frigid.

7. Zones.

The tropics and polar circles mark the earth off into belts or zones. Find them on the map.

Between the tropics — the hot or Torrid Zone.

Rainy and dry seasons. When? Why?

Between the tropics and polar circles — the two Temperate Zones.

Four seasons — The most favorable conditions for civilization.

Between the poles and polar circles — the two Arctic or Frigid Zones.

Short summers — long winters.

Lead pupils to *observe* the difference in the daily path of the sun, from month to month, and to report it. To observe also the difference in time and direction of the sun's rays coming through a school-room window at different seasons. Also the greater heat of noontide rays than of the morning or evening rays. Of summer than of winter rays.

Give or read some vivid description of the long winter night in northern regions, with its auroras, etc.; then the gradual return of the sun, — first a long twilight; then a peep of sunlight; then lengthening days, till the sun does not set. Then the gradual decline of sunlight into night again.

The poem "Bidding the Sun Good Night in Lapland," by Joy Allison, is appropriate here.

8. Difference in Time from Difference in Longitude.

Did you ever hear that a traveller finds his watch wrong when he arrives at a place east or west from his starting point?

We can now find out why this is so. Let us put a wafer on our globe where London is, another where we are. Put both places on the dark side. Rotate the globe. Raise your hands when the sun rises on one of these places — Which? Now the London clocks should show sunrise time. Should our clocks show time before or after sunrise?

If a watch, right for London time, were brought here, would it be too fast or too slow?

If a watch were carried from here to London, would it be too fast or too slow? Why?

Can we find out how much too slow or too fast these watches would be?

What do we know about the time of the earth's rotation?

What do we know about the number of degrees in every parallel?

What do we call distance east or west on the earth?

Who can solve this problem: If a place on any parallel rotates in 24 hours (makes the whole circle, or 360°), through how many degrees would it rotate in *one* hour?

Then how many degrees of longitude would make an hour's difference in time?

Now find for yourselves the difference in time between several places from the difference in their longitude.

Until recently, differences in the times of clocks and watches corresponded with differences in longitude; but, in these days of rapid travel over long railroad-lines, many people believe it desirable to keep the same time through fifteen degrees of longitude; thus making only four differences in time for our wide country. So we now have Eastern, Central, Mountain, and Pacific Time. This will be explained more fully later in the course. (See page 62.)

V. Winds — Currents of Air.

1. Why consider winds? Because they are the great modifiers of climate.

What is air?

We have an envelope of air (the atmosphere) around the earth, more than 100 miles deep. It differs in density — heavy near the earth — lighter as it is higher above the surface.

(Illustration — Difficulty in breathing on a high mountain.)

Air becomes lighter by taking watery vapor.

Barometer, as measure of pressure, or weight, of the air. As indicator of a storm coming.

Air becomes lighter (expands) by being heated.

(Illustration. — Hot air rising over a fire — upward draught.)

2. Why is the atmosphere restless? Why Winds?

Experiment. — Warm school-room — cool corridor — lighted candle held in the door-way. Candle at top of the door-way, flame blowing toward the corridor. Candle at bottom of the door-way, flame blowing toward the room.

Two currents of air in opposite directions; the lower a cold current — a surface-draught, or wind.

These currents are caused by a difference of temperature in the room and corridor. The hot air rises, and cold air flows in to supply its place.

3. Breezes at the Seashore in the Summer.

During the day the land and the air over it are hotter than the surface of the water and the air over it.

What kind of breeze? Sea breeze.

(*Note.* — Wind always named by the direction from which it blows.

During the night and early morning, a land breeze. Why?

Inference. — Winds are caused by difference of temperature.

Direction of wind shown by weather-vane, drifting clouds, smoke.

4. Trade-Winds. Origin. Direction.

What do we know about differences of temperature on the earth? What parts always hot? What parts always cold? What, then, can we say about currents of air?

Ans. Always currents of cold air blowing from the polar regions toward the equator. Always hot air rising over the hot regions, and passing off toward the cold regions.

If the earth did not rotate, these polar winds would blow in the direction of the meridians. But the atmosphere rotates with the earth — that over the polar parts, slowly; that over the hot parts, rapidly.

What happens, then, to a stream of air coming from the north polar region toward the equator? Can it move in a north and south line? *Ans.* It has less speed of rotation than the parts of the earth over which it passes, so it falls more and more behind the meridian on which it started. It falls westward, or blows more and more from the eastward, as places farther south rotate under it.

So it is successively a north, a northeast, and, in the torrid zone, an east wind.

What happens to a similar stream of air starting from the south polar regions?

Thus in the Torrid Zone there is a nearly constant east wind. Before the days of steam ships the world's commerce depended so much on this wind that it was named the *Trade-Wind*.

Think why the "Windward islands" and "Leeward islands" were so named by sailors.

5. Return Currents, or Counter Trades.

What becomes of the heated air that rises over the hot regions?

Where would air be needed?

Would this heated air, rising, be felt *on the surface* of the earth as a wind?

Would it get cooled? How? What then?

What would be its speed of rotation?

How, then, would it blow over the northern hemisphere? (Our pleasant southwest winds.)

How over the southern hemisphere?

These are sometimes called the *return trades*, or *counter trades*. These winds bring abundant moisture to Western Europe, to the Pacific coast of North America, and to the coast of Chili.

6. **Zone of Calms.**

>Over the most heated equatorial belt the air is constantly rising in an *upward* current.
>Would there be a surface wind?
>This, then, is the Zone of Calms that sailors dread. (Read from "The Ancient Mariner.")
>Sudden gusts, hurricanes, etc., occur, however, for the upper current is often disturbed.
>This zone does not correspond exactly with the equator, because the land-masses make the temperature the highest a little north of the equator. Its position varies somewhat with the season, following the apparent movement of the sun north and south.
>The strong ascending current, where the sun is nearly or quite vertical, carries much vapor high into the atmosphere, to be rapidly condensed, and to fall in heavy showers during a few hours of the day. Therefore, the middle of the rainy season, for places within the tropics, corresponds in time with the vertical sun.

7. **Monsoons. — Season-Winds.**

>During the northern summer the great land-masses of Southern Asia become so heated that the air rises, and currents blow from the Indian Ocean — called the *Southwest Monsoon*. During the southern summer the reverse happens, from the great heat of the African lands, and there is a *Northeast Monsoon*.
>These winds are felt in the northern part of the Indian Ocean and the adjacent parts of the Pacific.

8. **Variable Winds.**

>The temperate zones have frequent changes of winds, and the winds blow from every direction, as we know. The polar winds and the return currents are, however, the prevailing winds.

9. **Offices of Winds.**

>Winds as purifiers of the earth's surface.
>Winds as distributers of moisture.
>Winds as intercepted by mountain ranges. Condensation of moisture.

VI. Ocean-Currents.

> The-trade winds, the great evaporation within the tropics, and the difference of temperature between the equatorial and polar regions determine these.
>
> After teaching winds, the causes and course of the currents are easily taught. *Polar, Equatorial, Return Currents.*
>
> Under currents — their direction shown by moving icebergs.
>
> Trace on a map the currents of the different oceans.
>
> Show how they are turned from their natural courses and divided by striking the land.
>
> Show their advantages.
>
> Show effects of the Gulf Stream — climate of Western Europe, storms, fogs, driftwood.
>
> Take imaginary voyages, and let the class decide upon winds and currents that would help or hinder.

THE PHYSICAL GEOGRAPHY OF THE CONTINENTS.

The foundations for the study of physical geography having been laid, a class is ready to take up the examination of the physical character of each grand division. *Application should be made constantly* of the knowledge already gained of the distribution of solar heat; and of winds, currents, etc., as the modifiers of climate.

The comparison and contrast of the physical conditions of the different grand divisions will give the repetition necessary to make this fundamental knowledge permanent.

THE PHYSICAL GEOGRAPHY OF A GRAND DIVISION.
OUTLINE FOR THE STUDY.

I. Position on the Globe.
  Hemisphere.
  Zones.
  Crossed by what Circles? Where?
  Limits as to Latitude and Longitude.
 Position relative to other grand divisions.
  Surrounding Waters.
  Land Boundaries.

II. Size.
  Relative to the other grand divisions.
  Area — in round numbers.

III. Shape.
  General Form.
  Outline — regular or irregular. Compared with that of grand divisions previously studied.

METHODS OF TEACHING GEOGRAPHY. 47

Description of Coast. { Projections. / Indentations. / Border Islands.

Outline drawn as a part of the study of shape, not from memory at first.

Practice in Map-drawing as the study proceeds. When construction-lines are used let them be derived from the map, and let the climatic circles that cross the grand division appear on the map.

IV. Surface.

Highlands. { Primary. / Secondary. }
- Position of Mountain Systems.
- Direction.
- Ranges.
- Highest Peaks (see Note).
- Volcanoes.
- Plateaus. { Height / Extent (see Note). }
- Slopes.

(The relief is best studied by the use of a moulding-board.)

Lowlands. { Plains — fertile or desert. / Valleys. }

Striking Scenery.

Profiles drawn (from sections of the moulded form, at first).

Outline-map with Mountain Systems indicated upon it.

Comparison with the surface of grand divisions previously studied.

V. Drainage.

Water-partings and Water-sheds. { Direction. / Extent (see Note). }

River-basins. { Limits of. / Relative size (see Note). }

Principal Rivers.
- Source.
- Direction.
- Length (see Note).
- Main Stream and Tributaries.
- Mouth, Delta, Estuary, etc.
- Characteristics. { Navigable or not. / Scenery. }

NOTE. — (Memorize *very few* exact measurements. Compare others with these standards.)

Lakes. — Location. { Salt. / Fresh.

Outline-map with the principal Mountains, Rivers, and Lakes indicated upon it.

Comparison with the drainage of grand divisions already studied.

VI. Climate.

Temperature of different parts inferred from Position on the Earth.

Variation in Seasons, and in length of Days and Nights in the different parts.

Modifications of Climate { by Relief. / by Winds and Currents.

Moisture or Dryness of different parts.

Healthfulness of different parts.

Comparison of Coast with Interior as to climate.

Comparison with the climate of grand divisions already studied.

VII. Life.

Vegetable. { Wild, / Cultivated. } { Of different parts, inferred from climate.

Animal. { Wild, / Domestic. } Special for different regions. Peculiar to the grand division.

Human. { People of different parts. / Savage — Nomadic — Civilized.

Compared and contrasted with other grand divisions.

VIII. Regions adapted to —

Mining or Quarrying — Resources of each.

Agriculture or Grazing.

Manufactures.

Commerce or Trade. { Products that are exported, and products that are not exported, distinguished.

IX. Good Positions for important Cities — Natural Advantages of these Cities.

X. Topical Review — oral and written — with Map drawn from Memory.

A series of map-sketches, each illustrating one or two topics clearly, will be helpful in the review, and will give the practice needed to fix the map in the memory.

One outline may contain only the principal mountain-systems, rivers, and lakes, with their names.

Another, the names of projections and indentations of the coast-line, and of important seaports. Mountains and rivers, with inland cities, may be indicated, if desirable.

Another outline, for the names of important productions, — mineral, vegetable, animal.

POLITICAL GEOGRAPHY.

HAVING studied and compared the physical conditions of the grand divisions, a class is prepared to take the study of *the countries* of each, with special reference to the life of the inhabitants. Pupils can now be led to perceive that varied physical features give the opportunity for varied industries and for a higher degree of civilization. They will see that natural barriers are often the boundaries between countries.

This study of the people of the earth will naturally be preceded by the consideration of their division into *races, states of society*, different forms of *government* and *religion*, with the characteristics of each.

If the usual arrangement of text-books be followed, the detailed study of North America will be taken first; that of South America next; and lastly, the countries of the Old World will be studied. This seems, at first, the natural order; but, in this *Second Course* of Lessons, there are advantages in taking the study of the civil geography of the New World after that of Europe. When pupils have learned the national traits of Spaniards, Portuguese, Dutch, English, and French, they are interested in finding them transplanted into the lands that are or have been colonies of European nations. They will anticipate the social conditions in countries of the Western Hemisphere, and will readily trace for themselves the descent of the inhabitants by the names upon the maps.

We can easily lead them to see why the nations of Southern Europe were early navigators; how, naturally, the course

METHODS OF TEACHING GEOGRAPHY. 51

of discovery was along the African coast, till India, long known, had been reached by water (1498); and that the hope of reaching it, by sailing westward, had previously led Columbus to the discovery of America.

As the geography of countries is closely associated with the study of their history, so historical links should be made in studying political geography. Experience has proved that there is both economy of time and increase of interest for a class, when the special study of Europe precedes that of the political divisions of the New World. The following order of study is therefore suggested:—

The Countries (1) of Europe—(2) of North America—(3) of South America—(4) of Asia—(5) of Africa—(6) Australia; Malaysia, and other islands of the Pacific.

THE COUNTRIES OF A GRAND DIVISION.

METHOD OF STUDY.

I. **A General Review** of the Physical Features of the Grand Division, with Map-drawing from Memory.

II. **The Names, Relative Position, and Relative Size** of its Countries — Historical Points — Settlements.

III. **Study of a Country — Physical and Political.**

> Map-drawing of the Country, as the study proceeds. (In the manner indicated for the study of New England, in the first course, pp. 26, 27. With or without the use of a moulding-board.)
>
> Practice-maps will be important aids in the study and review.
>
> Memory-maps of the most important countries, and of sections of the United States, so far only as time will permit without abridging the descriptive geography.

Position in the Grand Division — Boundaries.
Character of the Coast-line, if any.

Surface.
- What Mountain-system, if any, crosses it?
- Ranges — High peaks — Scenery — Resources.
- Different kinds of Surface — Adapted to?
- Rivers — Lakes — Useful for?

Climate.
- As inferred from Position on the Earth.
- As modified by Relief, Winds, Ocean-Currents.
- Moisture, Dryness, Healthfulness — of different parts.
- Compared with that of the other countries of the grand division.

Vegetation — wild and cultivated — products of different parts.
Animal-life — wild and domestic — special or peculiar.

Inhabitants.
- Races — Languages — Government.
- Religion — Education — Customs and Manners.
- Occupations.
  - Agriculture — Staples.
  - Mining — Products.
  - Fishing.
  - Manufactures — Kinds of? Where?
- Trade and Commerce.
  - Exports — where sent?
  - Imports — where obtained?
- Population — where sparse — where crowded? Why?
- Important Cities and Towns — situation — natural advantages.
- Description of the most prominent city or cities.

For Review. — Take imaginary journeys, describing —
    the route;
    the scenery and resources of the region;
    the cities passed through.

Trace the great railroad lines, if any.
Other facilities for communication.
Take an imaginary journey for business.
Note important historical points — colonies — foreign possessions, if any.

METHODS OF TEACHING GEOGRAPHY. 53

The best way to review and strengthen the elementary knowledge of astronomical and physical geography, previously acquired, is to apply it, as the study of countries proceeds. Such of the following questions as are appropriate for any country will recall this knowledge.

> Does any part of this country have a vertical sun? If so, what part? Why?
> What do you know of the change of seasons in this country?
> Compare a winter and a summer day at ——— city.
> What other cities of the world (or what cities of countries recently studied) are in about the same latitude?
> How do they compare with this city in climate and industries?
> Do any of these cities have noon at about the same time?
> How does the time of day at ——— city compare with our time?
> Does any part of this country have the trade wind?
> What are the prevailing winds? Why?
> Which slope of the mountains has the more moisture? Why?
> Which plants, belonging to the zone, are not found in this country? Why?
> Which animals, belonging to the zone, are not found here? Why?

When the study of the Countries of a Grand Division is completed, the reading of one of the "Geographical Plays for Schools," by Miss Andrews, will give an excellent review, and will furnish material for topical recitation, oral and written.

The time given to the study of countries must depend upon their relative importance. Our own country and the countries of Europe will need more time than the countries of any other grand division.

A SKETCH FOR THE STUDY OF THE COUNTRIES OF AFRICA.
(In continuation of that given for the First Course.)

North Africa.

1. Boundaries — Countries — Coast-line. — Mountains along the coast, declining in height eastward. — Position, just north of the tropic of Cancer. — Climate, sub-tropical — wet and dry seasons — irrigation often necessary. — Date, gum, and cypress trees, and aromatic plants ("Land of dates"). — Lion, gazelle, hyena, jackal.

2. Some reference to the prominent place of North African nations in ancient times: half-buried pedestals (Carthage); hieroglyphics; pyramids; ruins of old Egyptian civilization. — Mohammed. — Conquest and permanent occupation of North Africa by Arabs. — Religion. — Koran. — Two Classes of Inhabitants: (1) dwellers in cities; (2) pastoral tribes. — Customs. — Caravans. — Description of Cairo, as a representative Mohammedan city, — architecture, bazaars, shops, baths, mosques, etc. (See Lane's "Modern Egyptians"; Bayard Taylor's "Lands of the Saracen.")

3. Barbary States — names — government — French possession of Algeria. Cities. — Few manufactures, — morocco and leather, silk and woollens. — Exports — oil, dates, nuts, sponge.

4. Valley of the Nile — course of the river — country during the overflow — irrigation by canals — villages — the whole population along the river. Products — grain, cotton, beans. No forests — clusters of palms around villages — lotus, papyrus, etc., in canals. Condition of the country people — government. (See "Egypt," by Stanley Lane-Poole; "Egypt and Nubia," by J. A. St. John.)

Suez-canal. — Late war in Egypt — causes of.

Sahara and Soudan.

1. Sahara — a vast desert, equal in area to the whole of Europe, extending across the continent, from the Atlantic to the Red Sea, interrupted only by the narrow strip fertilized by the Nile — large sandy tracts, rocky ridges, and a few oases. Crossed by the tropic, long under a vertical sun, with winds coming over the land to a warmer region and hence dry. Rainless, except where occasional elevations cool the air and condense the moisture. Around these heights, fertility and verdure. Caravans — Bedouins.

2. Soudan — the meeting-ground of Arabs and Negroes. — A great, open plain, fertile and populous, with ridges of hills, and a succession of shallow lakes or ponds often encrusted with natron (carbonate of soda), an important article of commerce. Patches of forest; pasture lands; tracts of wild rice, indigo, cotton, sugar-cane, millet, etc., with clusters of palms, acacias, tamarind-trees, and the great baobab. Herds of elephants, antelopes, and giraffes.

Provinces under Mohammedan governors — Many negro villages, and, across the country, a line of large cities, trading centres, in which the square, flat-roofed houses of the Arabs, and the round, thatched huts of the negroes, stand side by side. Description of Kano as a representative city. (See Barth, "Travels and Discoveries in North and Central Africa," Vol. III.; or Schweinfurth's "Heart of Africa.") The natives, the most advanced of the negro tribes, have a few manufactures; keep cattle; and cultivate a little cotton, grain, and manioc. Caravans from the North bring Arab clothing (shawls, bernouses, etc.), knives, guns, silk, and salt; and carry back natron, ivory, honey, wax, and slaves.

The Abyssinian Plateau — nominally independent.

Almost Unexplored Region.

1. South of Soudan, the equatorial region of trade-winds, rains, large rivers (Congo, the largest), and lakes (the head-waters of the Nile). Thick, tropical forests with lions, elephants, zebras, antelopes, rhinoceri. Numerous streams with crocodiles and hippopotami; swarms of locusts; mound-building termites; the tsetse-fly; and, among the hills, apes, gorillas, and other large species of the monkey tribe.

Farther south, areas of swamps and grass-lands subject to overflow; with scattered gum-trees, euphorbias, etc., in place of the rich, tropical forests.—Valley of the Zambesi river.

2. All this interior region inhabited by uncivilized tribes of negroes, and but little known.—Some account of recent explorers.—Condition and customs of natives—houses—occupations. (See Livingstone's "South Africa," and later books; Stanley's "Across the Dark Continent.")

A few well-known tribes; as Ashantees, Kaffirs, Hottentots.

West and East Coasts.

West Coast.—Mountain-chains,—not very high, parallel with the coast. A strip of low coast-lands, hot, moist, and unhealthful; with a desert-region, corresponding in position and cause to the desert of Atacama, in South America. Crossed by rivers, which deposit sand-bars at their mouths. Tall palms rise above the luxuriant forests and mangrove jungle on the river banks. — Rice, peanuts, sugar-cane, etc., cultivated; some coffee-plantations among the hills.— Thatched huts of the natives.—Small trading towns at intervals, chiefly Portuguese and English.—Senegambia, Sierra Leone, Liberia, Guinea, where?—Exports: oil, peanuts, gold-dust from the river-sands; with ivory, ostrich-feathers, and beeswax, brought by native traders from the interior.

East coast very much like the west, but Mohammedans, rather than English, in the towns. — The highest mountains along this coast.

South Africa.

The region of the tropic of Capricorn is marked by the Kalahari desert; long droughts; want of water.

South of Orange river, ridges running east and west. Tracts of "bush," or fleshy, spiny plants — aloes, etc.; also bulbous plants of great beauty, and a variety of heaths, — all characteristic of dry climates. — Upland grazing. — Community of Dutch Boers. — Gold and diamond mines. — Brief account of Portuguese discovery of the Cape of Good Hope. — Settlement by the Dutch. — Possession by the English. — Recent political troubles. — Ports. — Cape Town. — Elizabeth. — Grahamstown. — Exports: wool, wine, grain. — Description of towns, vegetation, animals, and modes of travel, "Cape-wagons." (See Livingstone's "South Africa," and "Seven Years in South Africa," by Dr. Holub.)

Commerce and Trade.

Commercial Routes. — 1. English steamers to Egypt and Suez Canal. — 2. French steamers between Marseilles and Algiers. — 3. United States trading-vessels to ports of West and South Coasts. — 4. Steamers and trading-vessels between England and Cape Colony. — 5. Trading-vessels from India and Arabia to East Coast, chiefly to ports of Zanzibar.

Inland Trade. — 1. Caravans between the fertile provinces of Soudan and the Mediterranean ports. — 2. Short lines of railway along the coast of South Africa, and trains of ox-wagons inland. — 3. In the interior, where the tsetse-fly is fatal to cattle, parties of native porters march single file, carrying on their heads loads of merchandise to and from the coast towns.

NOTE. — For other books on Africa, see List, pp. 69-71.

GENERAL REVIEW,

WITH FURTHER ATTENTION TO IMPORTANT POINTS.

When the countries of the earth have been studied, in the manner suggested, a class should have gathered facts enough concerning both physical and civil geography to make a final consideration of the whole subject both interesting and instructive.

This review should be, not so much a rehearsal of knowledge already acquired, as a comparison and classification of that knowledge, during which new points will be presented and new inferences made.

Such a review will naturally begin with the relation of our earth to the solar system, or with

Astronomical Geography.

More or less of the points here suggested can be taught, according to the interest and preparation of the class. Whether or not they are taught, a teacher of geography should be familiar with them.

If the whole conception is clear to the teacher, these points can be very simply presented. In some grammar schools all these points are taught with great clearness, and are responded to by classes with much interest. Such teaching gives to the many pupils, who do not go on to the study of astronomy in higher schools, a life-long habit of observing the daily and yearly phenomena of the heavens. Like all conceptions that are based upon observation, these points are most readily received by pupils who have not passed beyond the grammar-school age, and they are therefore the surest foundation for advanced study. The memorizing of facts and dependence upon diagrams, without the conception by the pupils of the celestial phenomena caused by the earth's motions, will result only in confusion.

Note —
>   The *relative* position and sizes of the planets, taking the earth as a standard.
>   The supposed condition of the sun, as the source of light and heat, and of the stars.
>   The former belief that the earth was at rest in the centre, and the apparent motions real.
>   The terms poles, axis, parallels, equator, as belonging to a rotating sphere. *Poles*, the two opposite stationary points. A line connecting these points, the *axis*. *Parallels*, circles described around the axis by points of the surface. *Equator*, the middle and largest parallel.
>   Observations of the apparent movements of sun, moon, and stars to be encouraged, and to be reported upon from time to time.

A class will be able to pass from the simple illustrations already given of the earth's motions and of their effects (pp. 26-32), to the conception of the imaginary celestial sphere, and of the apparent movements upon its concave surface. Such questions as these may lead to it: —

> If we should stand where our horizon was unbroken, how would the sky appear to us?
> Where would a person stand to see the other celestial hemisphere?
> Then if the earth did not intercept our view, we could see sky in all directions, or the whole concave surface of the celestial sphere.
> Imagine a vertical line extended to meet this celestial sphere — the points of meeting would be our *zenith* and our *nadir*. Point to the zenith (*up*) — the nadir (*down*).
> Draw the horizon-circle in the air.

Imagine the earth's axis prolonged to meet the celestial sphere.

Suppose an observer at the north pole of the earth — where would the prolonged axis meet his celestial sphere? What star would be in his zenith? Then his zenith would be the north point of the celestial sphere.

Suppose an observer at the equator — where would the pole-star be?

Suppose an observer 10° north of the equator — where would he see the pole-star?

Where in our sky is the pole-star?

Then to what does its altitude correspond?

Imagine the plane of our semi-meridian extended to the sky. How would it meet the sky?

Describe the celestial meridian, in the air, passing from the north point of the horizon, through the pole-star and the zenith, to the south point of the horizon.

Imagine the plane of the earth's equator extended to the sky — how much of the celestial equator is above our horizon? On which side of the zenith does it cross our meridian? How far from the zenith?

Describe it in the air, beginning at the east point of the horizon.

Think of the tropic of Cancer in relation to the equator — describe its position, if its plane were extended to meet our sky. The same for the tropic of Capricorn.

On what circle of the celestial sphere does the sun apparently move on the 21st of March?

Then describe the sun's path to an observer on the equator, on that day.

Describe the sun's path through our sky on that day.

When does the sun apparently move over the tropic of Cancer?

Describe his path through our sky on that day.

Describe his path through our sky when vertical at the tropic of Capricorn.

Describe the sun's daily path at each of these dates from different points of observation — on or near the equator — on or near the north pole — on the Arctic circle.

During what part of the year does the sun rise north of the east point and set north of the west point of our horizon?

South of the east and west points?

Describe the movement of the sun during the period of continuous day just north of the Arctic circle — the different place of the mid-day and midnight sun. The different place of the rising and setting sun through the year.

Illustrate the greater heat of rays falling vertically than of rays falling obliquely — more rays on a given space, less atmosphere traversed, when falling vertically.

Show difference in direction of noontime-rays and of morning or evening rays. Of noontime-rays in summer and winter. — Inferences.

When pupils inquire *why* it is cold on a high mountain near the equator, under a vertical sun, they are ready to learn, —
> That rays of heat are felt only when they meet substances to be affected by them.
> That the earth's atmosphere, and its surface of land and water, receive heat.
> That space beyond the earth's atmosphere is believed to be cold.
> That persons ascending mountains or in balloons find it colder and darker as they reach greater heights and leave more and more of the earth's atmosphere below them.

When pupils ask, "Why, as the sun is so much larger than the earth, its rays do not come round the earth to us at night?" they need to learn, —
> That light is not a visible substance, but only a means of sight.
> That objects become visible when they receive rays of light and send them to our eyes.
> That our atmosphere receives and sends us light, otherwise we should have no diffused daylight, but a bright sun in a dark sky.
> That, at midnight, when the sun is far below the horizon, the rays still shoot up all round the earth, *into the space beyond our atmosphere*, but give us no light unless they fall upon the moon or a planet, and are reflected to our eyes.
> That, for a time before sunrise and after sunset, we have *twilight*, or light from the upper regions of our atmosphere, which receive the sun's rays earlier and later than they can reach us.

Find the cause of the long twilight in high latitudes.
Describe midwinter in high latitudes, auroras, moonlight, etc.

The sun's apparent course among the stars during a year marks a great circle on the celestial sphere, inclined 23½° to the celestial equator, and called the *ecliptic*, because eclipses occur if the moon, when new or full, is on or near this circle.

The sun's apparent movement north and south of the equator, as it becomes vertical to every place within the tropics, is called its motion in *declination*. This corresponds to latitude on the earth. (See almanac for sun's declination at any time.)

State clearly the *three causes* of the sun's apparent motion through a year.

Explain this familiar statement: "The sun is crossing the line."

Describe the sun's apparent motion in declination from March 20th to June 21st. From June to September.

Terms *equinox* and *solstice* — how applied?

The sun is said to be in the signs Aries, Cancer, Capricorn, etc. (See almanac.) What is meant?

NOTE. — Joslin's "Solar Telluric Globe" illustrates these points and many others very clearly.

Relations of Time to Longitude.

Pupils now understand that rotation brings all the meridians under the sun every twenty-four hours, or that noon travels westward round the earth, at the rate of 15° in an hour.

Mariners sailing westward round the earth lose a day; and sailing eastward gain a day. They must correct their reckoning in each case.

By common consent, sailors now change their day in longitude 180° from Greenwich. This meridian passes over the Pacific ocean, and crosses scarcely any land; so it is a convenient longitude for the change of day.

Give practice in determining the difference in local time at two places; their difference in longitude being given and *vice versâ*.

"Standard Time." — Hourly standards recently adopted. — Advantages to railroad managers and travellers.

North America divided into five sections, each 15° wide. The 60th, 75th, 90th, 105th, 120th meridians, the middle lines of these sections. The same public time throughout a section. The five hourly standards designated respectively Intercolonial, Eastern, Central, Mountain, Pacific Time.

METHODS OF TEACHING GEOGRAPHY. 63

The greatest possible difference between local time and standard time, half an hour, at places on the borders of the sections. The difference between the standard time of neighboring places on opposite sides of a section line, one hour.

The Eastern Time meridian passes between New York and Philadelphia, and the Central Time meridian between Chicago and St. Louis. Therefore, in these centres of population, local time and standard time practically coincide.

The Tidal Wave.

A result of rotation, and of the unequal attraction of the sun and moon on different parts of the earth.

The moon the chief tide-producing force. Particles of water free to respond to the attracting force; hence the tidal wave.

Spring tides occur when?
Neap tides occur when? Why?

The form of the coast-line as affecting the height and time of the tide. — Examples.

Winds — Ocean-Currents — Climate — Flora — Fauna.

If the elementary knowledge of these topics has been applied, as the study of the grand divisions has proceeded, pupils will be ready now for a more general treatment of them.

Let the class trace long voyages, and decide where the winds and currents would be favorable, and where unfavorable. What changes of climate would be met.

Follow the course of famous explorers, and inquire into the different physical conditions they found.

Compare climates in the same latitudes, and show why isothermal lines do not correspond with the parallels.

Consider the effect of climate upon the life of the inhabitants of different countries.

Show that the height of the line of perpetual snow on mountains varies with the latitude.

Find the geographical distribution of useful plants and animals.

Compare the vegetation and animals of different grand divisions within the tropics. Account for the contrasts.

Mark out belts of vegetation, corresponding with the distribution of heat and moisture. These broadly stated, and with many local exceptions, are —

> An equatorial forest-belt, on both sides of the equator, in a region of great heat and moisture.
>
> A desert-belt, corresponding with each tropic, where the sun is vertical longer than elsewhere, and there is much dryness with the great heat.
>
> A transition region of pasture or grass-lands, between these belts, in each hemisphere.
>
> Another transition region of grass-lands, in each hemisphere, beyond the desert-belts.
>
> A temperate forest-belt, in each hemisphere, where the return trades prevail. A great variety of deciduous trees, the species varying with the increasing latitude.
>
> A belt of mosses and lichens in each hemisphere, between the temperate forests and the polar regions of ice and snow.

Trace the correspondence in vegetation between the base and summit of a high mountain in the torrid zone, and between the equator and the poles.

The representation on outline maps of the direction of winds and currents, of the place of important productions, characteristic animals, etc., will be the surest means of fixing this knowledge, though there will not be time for much memory-work of this kind. One outline for climatic lines, another for direction of winds, another for productions, etc., will give clear impressions, which cannot be gained from published maps where all these points are crowded within one outline.

The Work of Water.

On the Surface and Underground.

> Review and enlarge the early observation-lessons on evaporation, condensation, mist, fog, clouds (different kinds), rain.

The distribution of rain depends upon the physical features of a country and the prevailing winds. Mountain-sides receive much rain, because the air, blowing up the slope, is chilled and deposits its moisture. Many mountains have a moist and a dry side, according to the direction of the wind. Table-lands surrounded by mountains have little rain.

What becomes of the rain? Part of it flows off into the streams and rivers. Part of it sinks below the surface. The underground rain-water sinks through porous soils (sand-beds, sandstones, etc.) and through cracks in the rocks; but it cannot penetrate clay-beds, etc., and flows along underground till it finds an outlet and forms a spring.

Rain, falling through the atmosphere, takes up carbonic acid gas from the air (we breathe it into the air), and carries it underground, where it helps to dissolve (we say acids eat) the mineral substances, and thus we have mineral-springs.

The salt of the sea comes from the salt dissolved out of the rocks.

Underground water forms caves by gradually dissolving the rock-particles and removing them.

Rain, flowing over the ground, dissolves the rock-particles, and the surface-rocks gradually crumble into soil. Rain-water, freezing in the rocks, makes them crack. We get soil from the surface-rocks mainly by the action of water. Different rocks make different soils, some more fertile than others. Plants, growing in and decaying on the soil, help to form more soil.

> Observations of a wayside-pool and of a hillside road, after a heavy shower, will give many points.

Water finds out the lowest levels, all the irregularities of the surface, and brooks and rivers deepen their own channels.

Rock-material is carried by rivers to the sea. Terraces, deltas, ravines, and cañons are formed by the action of water.

The coast-line is changed by the action of waves and tides. Cliffs, bays, and caverns are the effects.

Glaciers and Icebergs.

Perpetual snow-fields. — Motion down the slopes. — The pressed snow formed into ice.
River of ice (glacier) moving down the high valley.
River flowing from the melted end of the ice.
Moraines. — Crevasses. — Rock-scratches.
Icebergs. — Masses of ice broken from the ends of glaciers which reach the coast.

Coral Islands and Reefs.

In the torrid zone, chiefly in the Pacific ocean; but there are many in the Indian ocean and in the region of the West Indies. Large reefs near Florida and Australia.

Formed mainly by the united skeletons of myriads of coral-polyps, but partly by the action of the waves.

>Coral the result of growth, not of building.
>Description of a polyp. Of a colony.
>Mode of growth. Material for coral separated from sea-water by the polyps.
>Fringing reefs. Barrier reefs.
>Atolls — formed around island-mountains — and therefore usually oval or circular in form. Gradual sinking of the sea-bottom till the island is submerged. Thus a Lagoon, with an encircling reef.
>Different kinds of polyps form different kinds of coral, at different heights of a reef.
>Work of the waves when a reef reaches the surface of the water.
>First vegetation — Flora and Fauna of coral islands.
>Specimens. Illustrations.

Volcanoes and Earthquakes.

Formation of a volcanic mountain.
Phenomena of eruptions. Materials ejected.
Trace the lines of volcanic action, and connect their **nearness** to the ocean with the present theory of volcanic action.
Phenomena of earthquakes.
Probable connection between volcanoes and earthquakes.

METHODS OF TEACHING GEOGRAPHY. 67

Changes on the Earth's Surface.

By *water in motion*, — waves, tides, currents, rivers, glaciers, — causing erosion, débris, transportation of rocks.

By *winds, drifting sands*, etc.

By *vegetation* and *animal life* (coral islands).

By *volcanoes* and *earthquakes*.

Distribution of Land and Water.

Land hemisphere — London about the centre.

Water hemisphere — New Zealand about the centre.

Northern hemisphere more land than water, the continents pointing southward.

Old World stretching from east to west, nearly half round the globe. Mountain-framework in the same direction.

New World extending north and south. Mountain-framework in the same direction.

> Inference — General outline corresponds to direction of mountain-systems. (Draw mountain-systems of a grand division.)

Old World — vast northern plains.

New World — vast central plains.

The Oceans.

Comparative size and importance.

Bordering countries.

Character of the ocean-bed. Soundings.

Icebergs. Sargasso Sea.

Life in the ocean.

Commercial products.

Main routes of ocean-commerce.

Winds and currents as favoring or hindering voyages.

Islands classified. { Continental. Oceanic. Volcanic. Coral.

The Grand Divisions compared as to

Coast-line — navigable rivers and lakes — climate.

Agricultural regions and their products.

Manufacturing regions and their products.

Mining regions and their products.
Distribution of races of men.
The great routes for trade and commerce traced.
The probable cargoes of vessels from important points given.

The Course of Discovery and the Progress of Civilization.

These topics will be specially interesting at the close of the study of the earth as the home of man — noting,

The early civilizations in the valleys of the Nile, Tigris, and Euphrates.
The early but isolated nations of India and China.
Grecian and Roman civilization.
Pyramids, ruins of temples, palaces, etc., as evidences of early civilization.
Physical conditions for the spread of civilization in Europe — temperate climate, varied coast-line, accessible interior.
Different nationalities in Europe.
Wonderful spread of Mohammedanism.
The Crusades. — Effects.
Marco Polo's travels, bringing knowledge of Asia.
Early maritime nations — Genoese — Portuguese.
Discoveries on the coast of Africa. Prince Henry of Portugal.
Search for a passage to India.
Columbus — The New World.
Vasco da Gama — Ocean-route to India.
Magellan's circumnavigation.
Cortes and Pizarro — Ancient civilization in the New World.
English, Dutch, and French discoveries and colonies.
Russian America (Alaska).
Cook's Voyages. Arctic Voyages. Explorations in Africa.
Present colonial possessions of different nations.
Recent Japanese civilization.
Present facilities for communication throughout the civilized world.

A LIST OF BOOKS,

IN ADDITION TO THOSE REFERRED TO IN THE NOTES, THAT HAVE BEEN FOUND USEFUL IN TEACHING GEOGRAPHY.

Science Primer, — Physical Geography — *Geikie.*
History Primer, — Geography — *Grove.*
Science Ladder, No. 1, Forms of Land and Water — *D'Anvers.*
The Fairy Land of Science — *Arabella B. Buckley.*
Physiography — *Huxley.*
Earth and Man — *Guyot.*
Physical Geography. Revised edition — *Maury.*
Elements of Physical Geography — *Geikie.*
The Earth, Ocean, Atmosphere, and Life (2 vols.) *Réclus.*
Geological Sketches — *Agassiz.*
Glaciers (Illustrated quarto) — *Shaler & Davis.*

Science Primer, — Astronomy (pp. 1–40) — *Lockyer.*
A Mathematical Geography for Common Schools — *Jackson.*
Astronomy for Schools and General Readers (pp. 92–100) — *Sharpless & Philips.*
A Hand-Book of the Terrestrial Globe (pp. 12–54) — *Ellen C. Fitz.*

> (The last four books present a simple treatment of the motions of the Earth and their effects.)

What Mr. Darwin saw in his Voyage round the World — Published by *Harper & Brothers.*
Round the World, by a Boy — *Smiles.*
Around the World — *Prime.*
The Polar and Tropical World — *Hartwig.*
The Sea and its Living Wonders — *Hartwig.*
The Subterranean World — *Hartwig.*
Geography, Physical, Historical, Descriptive — *Keith Johnston.*

Compendium of Geography and Travels (6 vols., illustrated) — Published by *Stanford*.
The Countries of the World (6 vols., illustrated, one for each Grand Division) — *Robert Brown*.
Wanderings in Four Continents — Published by *Lippincott & Co*.

Manual of Commerce — *S. W. Browne*.
Science Primer, — Natural Resources of the United States — *Patton*.
A Hand-Book to the Industries of the British Isles and the United States — *Bevan*.
Commercial Products of the Sea — *Simmonds*.
The Geography of the Oceans (containing Tables of Commerce) — *J. F. Williams*.
The Statesman's Year Book, Statistical and Historical Annual of the States of the Civilized World — Published by *Macmillan & Co*.

Arctic Explorations — *Kane*.
Open Polar Sea — *Hayes*.
Alaska — *Dall*.
Oregon Trail — *Parkman*.
Wonders of the Yellowstone — *Richardson*.
Colorado — *Bayard Taylor*.
The West — *Robert P. Porter*.
Nooks and Corners of the New England Coast — *Drake*.
Journey in Brazil — *Agassiz*.
Up the Amazon and Madeira Rivers — *Matthews*.
The Pampas and Andes, A Thousand Miles' Walk Across South America — *N. H. Bishop*.
Between the Amazon and Andes, or Journey Across the Pampas — *Mrs. Mulhall*.
Life and Nature under the Tropics (Orinoco, Amazon, Andes) — *Myers*.

Mr. Bodley Abroad — *Scudder*.
The Bodleys in Holland — *Scudder*.
Zigzag Journeys (5 vols.) — *Butterworth*.
Boy Travellers in the Far East (4 vols.) — *Knox*.
Our Young Folks Abroad — *McCabe*.
Our Young Folks in Africa — *McCabe*.
A Family Flight (3 vols.) — *Hale*.

METHODS OF TEACHING GEOGRAPHY. 71

Northern Travel (Sweden) — *Bayard Taylor.*
Land of the Midnight Sun — *Du Chaillu.*
The Alhambra — *Irving.*
The Albert Nyanza — *Baker.*
Land Journey through Siberia — *Collins.*
Oriental and Western Siberia — *Atkinson.*
Travels in the Region of the Amoor — *Atkinson.*
Overland through Asia, or Pictures of Tartar Life — *Knox.*
The Middle Kingdom, or Chinese Empire — *S. Wells Williams.*
China — *Douglas.*
Arabia — *Bayard Taylor.*
English Governess in Siam — *Mrs. A. H. Leonowens.*
Malay Archipelago — *Wallace.*

Various Text-Books, Guide-Books, Hand-Books, Geographical Readers, and selections from works of Fiction (as descriptive passages from Bulwer's Last Days of Pompeii, etc.).

The wide range of Photographic Illustrations, made possible by the introduction of the Solar Camera into our school-rooms, adds greatly to the value and interest of lessons in descriptive geography.

Educational and Geographical Works.

GLOBES.

BOSTON SCHOOL SUPPLY COMPANY,
Wholesale Educational Booksellers, Importers, and General School Furnishers,
JOHN A. BOYLE, Manager.   15 BROMFIELD STREET, BOSTON.

BOSTON SCHOOL SUPPLY CO.

JOSLIN'S
Terrestrial and Celestial
GLOBES.

Gold and Silver Medals and Diplomas have been awarded for these Globes in New York, Philadelphia, Boston, and Baltimore, and whenever other Globes have been placed in competition, these have invariably obtained the highest award.

USEFULNESS OF GLOBES.

The importance of Globes, both as articles of school and household furniture, has long been greatly under-estimated.

Until within a few years they were to be found only among our colleges and leading academies, with occasionally one in some public or private library, and were regarded almost in the light of a curiosity by the large masses of people.

In these days of popular education, however, the importance and necessity of their use in framing correct ideas in the minds of children has become much more widely recognized, and has led to their general introduction into schools of all grades.

The presence of a Globe in the school-room has been found to be of the greatest assistance; having it constantly before them, the scholars acquire correct ideas which could not be gathered from books.

As an example of the increased consideration now being given to this subject, we may say that the City of Boston, whose schools are universally conceded to be among the foremost in this country, has purchased for their use *one or more of Joslin's Globes for every school-room above the primary grade throughout the city*. Moreover, the Joslin Globe was selected after a critical examination by the Committee of all globes in the market.

Some of the advantages of Joslin's Globes are: They may be depended upon as *accurate*, the plates having lately been revised to correspond with all recent political changes. All the maps are printed *directly from copper plates*, and are not lithographed. The meridians are *accurately graduated*. *The varnish is warranted not to crack or peel off*, a common failing. The stands are thoroughly and firmly fitted together, and the *general workmanship throughout* is of the *first order*.

It will be the constant endeavor of the maker to maintain the reputation of the globes for superior accuracy, durability, and beauty, and to merit on that account a liberal share of public patronage.

Finally, as the JOSLIN GLOBE is the only make that we CAN WARRANT in every particular, therefore we handle and SELL NO OTHER.

BOSTON SCHOOL SUPPLY CO. -
15 Bromfield Street, Boston.

BOSTON SCHOOL SUPPLY CO.

Style 1.
Joslin's Bronze Pedestal Stand.

JOSLIN'S
BRONZE PEDESTAL STAND.

STYLE 1.

Mounted in this manner, the globe is brought to a convenient height for use while sitting, and, at the same time, presents an ornamental appearance adapting it to the parlor and library, as well as to the school-room. It is furnished with horizon, graduated full brass nickel-plated meridian, hour dial, etc.

The stand is of bronzed iron, and of such design as to combine great strength with light weight and symmetrical appearance. Being mounted upon brass castors, can be readily moved to any position.

PRICES:

18-inch Globe, 43 inches high $64.00
16   "   "   42½ "   " 50.00
12   "   "   38½ "   " 30.00

Globe with Celestial Map, same price.

BOSTON SCHOOL SUPPLY CO.

Style 2.
Joslin's Tripod Stand.

JOSLIN'S TRIPOD STAND.

STYLE 2.

This style of mounting was gotten up particularly for parlor and library use, many persons objecting to an iron stand. It makes a very light, strong, and ornamental stand, and will look well with any furniture. The arms that support the ball and horizon are japanned and decorated, and pivoted the same as in all rotary globes. The legs are japanned with a little decorating, and screw into the socket supporting the arms by a polished brass cap-piece fastened to their top.

PRICES:

18 inch Globe $62.50
16 "   " 48.00
12 "   " 30.00

Globe with Celestial Map, same price.

BOSTON SCHOOL SUPPLY CO.

JOSLIN'S LOW BRONZE STAND.

STYLE 3.

This style, with black walnut horizon, graduated full brass meridian, hour dial, etc., is mounted upon a light bronzed stand of neat and appropriate design.

The arms which support the horizon are pivoted to the base, thus allowing any portion of the globe to be turned to the student without changing the position of the base itself, — a very desirable arrangement.

PRICES:

16 inch Globe	$40.00
12 " "	20.00
10 " "	14.50

Globe with Celestial Map, same price.

BOSTON SCHOOL SUPPLY CO.

Joslin's Full Wood Stand.

STYLE 4.

Mounted upon a substantially made cherry wood stand, with horizon, graduated full brass meridian, hour dial, and index, this globe has all the appliances for use in the solution of problems.

It is well adapted to all grades of schools.

PRICES:

16 inch Globe	$36.00
12 " "	17.60
10 " "	13.60
6 " "	8.00

Globe with Celestial Map, same price.

BOSTON SCHOOL SUPPLY CO.

JOSLIN'S LOW TRIPOD STAND.

STYLE 5.

Mounted upon three light, neat, bronzed iron legs, (preventing any shrinking and coming apart, as sometimes happens in wooden stands), with black walnut horizon, graduated full brass meridian, hour dial, and index. Everything is as accurate as in the highest priced globe ever made.

PRICES:

12 inch Globe	$17.60
10 " "	13.60

Globe with Celestial Map, same price.

BOSTON SCHOOL SUPPLY CO.

JOSLIN'S SEMI-CIRCLE STAND.

STYLE 6.

Polished black walnut stand, with graduated brass semi-meridian. For those who use the globe for reference only, and who never desire to work problems, this style is neat and most appropriate.

PRICES:

12 inch Globe	$13.60
10 " "	9.60
6 " "	4.00

Globe with Celestial Map, same price.

BOSTON SCHOOL SUPPLY CO.

JOSLIN'S
Telluric Globe.

This style was specially designed to furnish a *simple* means of illustrating the causes of the Changes of the Seasons and of the numerous other phenomena which are related to them. Their success in accomplishing this much desired end is fully attested by the high commendations of teachers from all sections of the country.

Each globe is accompanied with a printed manual of 30 pages, giving a complete description of the globe and its various uses, with illustrative problems.

PRICE:

6 inch Globe $15.00

Educational and Geographical Works.

ATLASES.

BOSTON SCHOOL SUPPLY COMPANY,
Wholesale Educational Booksellers, Importers, and General School Furnishers,
JOHN A. BOYLE, Manager.   15 BROMFIELD STREET, BOSTON.

BOSTON SCHOOL SUPPLY CO.

PHILIPS'

IMPERIAL ATLAS.

A series of New and Authentic Maps, size 22x32, engraved from Original Drawings, compiled from National Surveys, and the works of eminent Travellers and Explorers. Accompanied by a valuable Consulting Index of 120,000 names.

CONTENTS.

1. The World, in Hemispheres.
2. The World, on Mercator's Projection.
3. Europe.
4. British Empire, on a uniform scale.
5. Commercial and Industrial Map of the British Islands.
6. England and Wales (North).
7.   Do.   (South).
8. Scotland (North).
9.   Do.   (South).
10. Ireland (North).
11.   Do.   (South).
12. France.
13. Holland and Belgium.
14. Switzerland.
15. German Empire (North).
16.   Do.   (South).
17. Austro-Hungarian Empire.
18. Prussia.
19. Denmark, with the Foreign Possessions of the Danish Monarchy.
20. Sweden and Norway.
21. Russia in Europe.
22. Turkey in Europe.
23. Greece, the Ionian Islands, and the Archipelago.
24. Italy (North).
25.   Do. (South).
26. Spain and Portugal.
27. Asia.
28. Turkey in Asia.
29. Palestine and the Sinai Peninsula.
30. Arabia, with Egypt, Nubia, and Abyssinia.
31. Persia and Afghanistan.
32. India (North).
33.   Do. (South).
34. Burmah, Siam, Anam, and the East Indian Archipelago.
35. Chinese Empire and Japan.
36. Russia in Asia.
37. Africa.
38. Northern and Southern Africa.
39. North America.
40. Dominion of Canada (East).
41.   Do.   (West).
42. United States (North-Eastern).
43.   Do.   (Western).
44.   Do.   (South-Eastern).
45. Mexico and Central America.
46. West Indies.
47. South America (North).
48.   Do.   (South).
49. Australia (General Map).
50. New South Wales, Victoria, and South Australia.
51. New Zealand; and the Polynesian Islands.

Imperial Folio, Half-bound Russia, gilt edges.   Price, **$37.00**.

BOSTON SCHOOL SUPPLY CO.

PHILIPS'
General Atlas of the World.

A series of New and Authentic Maps, size 22x32, from Original Drawings, delineating the Natural and Political Divisions of the Empires, Kingdoms, and States of the World. Accompanied by a valuable Consulting Index of 90,000 names.

CONTENTS.

1. The World, in Hemispheres.
2. The World, on Mercator's Projection.
3. Europe.
4. British Empire, on a uniform scale.
5. Commercial and Industrial Map of the British Islands.
6. England and Wales.
7. Scotland.
8. Ireland.
9. France.
10. Holland and Belgium.
11. Switzerland.
12. German Empire.
13. Austro-Hungarian Empire.
14. Prussia.
15. Denmark, with the Foreign Possessions of the Danish Monarchy.
16. Sweden and Norway.
17. Russia in Europe.
18. Turkey in Europe.
19. Greece, the Ionian Islands, and the Archipelago.
20. Italy.
21. Spain and Portugal.
22. Asia.
23. Turkey in Asia.
24. Syria and the Sinai Peninsula.
25. India.
26. Burmah, Siam, Anam, and the East Indian Archipelago.
27. Chinese Empire and Japan.
28. Africa.
29. North America.
30. Canada, New Brunswick, Nova Scotia, and Newfoundland.
31. United States — North-Eastern Sheet.
32. United States — Western Sheet.
33. United States — South-Eastern Sheet.
34. Mexico and Central America.
35. West India Islands.
36. South America.
37. Australia — General Map.
38. New South Wales, Victoria, Queensland, and South Australia.
39. New Zealand and the Polynesian Islands.

Imperial Folio, Half-bound Morocco, gilt edges. Price, $22.00.

BOSTON SCHOOL SUPPLY CO.

PHILIPS'
Handy Atlas of the World.

A comprehensive series of Maps, size 15x19 inches, illustrating Modern, Historical, and Physical Geography. With a complete Consulting Index.

CONTENTS.

1. The World, on Sir John Herschel's Projection.
1a. North and South Polar Charts.
1b. Sketch-Map of the British Empire throughout the World.
2. The World in Hemispheres.
3. Map of the World.
3a. Physical Chart of the World.
4. Europe.
5. British Isles, North Sea.
6. England and Wales.
7. Scotland.
8. Ireland.
9. France.
10. German Empire.
11. Switzerland and the Alps.
12. Austro-Hungary.
13. Italy, Turkey in Europe, and Greece.
14. Spain and Portugal.
15. Sweden, Norway, Denmark, and the Baltic Sea.
16. Russia in Europe.
17. Asia.
18. Turkey in Asia, Persia, Arabia, Egypt.
19. Palestine, Ancient and Modern.
20. India, Afghanistan, Beloochistan, Burmah, and Siam.
21. Chinese Empire, Eastern Turkestan, etc.
21a. Japan, Liu Kiu Islands, and Formosa.
22. Africa.
23. North America.
24. Dominion of Canada and Northern United States.
25. United States.
26. Mexico, Central America, West India Islands, Colombia, and Venezuela.
27. South America.
28. Australia.
29. New South Wales, Victoria, and Part of South Australia.
30. Queensland.
31. New Zealand.
32. Oceania and the Pacific Ocean.
33. Minor British Possessions and Settlements in Europe, Africa, and adjoining Ocean.
34. Cape Colony and Natal.
35. Minor British Possessions in Asia.
36. British Possessions in America, and the Canadian Province of British Columbia.
37. The World as known to the Ancients.
38. Europe in the Eighteenth Century, previous to the French Revolution.
39. Europe during the earlier years of the Nineteenth Century, showing the Empire of Napoleon I.

Crown Folio, Half-bound Morocco, gilt edges. Price, $11.00.

BOSTON SCHOOL SUPPLY CO.

PHILIPS'
Popular Atlas of the World,

A Series of Thirty-six Maps, size 15x19, constructed from the most recent authorities. The Maps beautifully printed in colors.

Accompanied by a copious Consulting Index.

₊ The Popular Atlas embodies a selection of Maps eminently suited for general use, including all that are required for reference by the current necessities of the time; they form, in short, an epitome of Map knowledge — attractive in form, compendious in character, and moderate in price.

1. The World. On Sir John Herschel's Projection.
2. The World in Hemispheres.
3. Map of the World. Illustrating the Natural Productions of Different Lands.
3A. Physical Chart of the World. Illustrating the Distribution of Winds and the Principal Hydrographic Basins.
4. Europe and the Mediterranean Sea.
5. British Isles, North Sea, and Adjoining Countries.
6. England and Wales.
7. Scotland.
8. Ireland.
9. France.
10. German Empire.
10A. Belgium and the Netherlands.
11. Switzerland and the Alps.
12. Austria-Hungary.
13. Italy, Turkey in Europe, and Greece.
14. Spain and Portugal.
15. Sweden, Norway, Denmark, and the Baltic Sea.
16. Russia in Europe.
17. Asia.
18. Turkey in Asia, Persia, Arabia, Egypt, and the Countries of the Nile.
19. Palestine, Ancient and Modern.
20. India, Afghanistan, Beloochistan, Burmah, and Siam.
21. Chinese Empire.
22. Africa. Plan of Suez Canal and Delta of the Nile.
23. North America.
24. Dominion of Canada (Eastern Portion), and Northern United States.
25. United States.
26. Mexico, Central America, West India Islands, Columbia, and Venezuela.
27. South America.
28. Australia.
29. New South Wales, Victoria, and part of South Australia.
30. Queensland.
30A. Western Australia.
31. New Zealand.
32. Oceania and the Pacific Ocean.
33. Minor British Possessions and Settlements in Africa, and Adjoining Oceans, with Cyprus.
34. Cape Colony and Natal.
35. Transvaal and Orange Free State.
36. Minor British Possessions in America, and the Canadian Province of British Columbia.

Crown Folio, half-bound, gilt edges, price $7.35.

BOSTON SCHOOL SUPPLY CO.

PHILIPS'
Atlas of Physical Geography.

In a Series of beautifully engraved Maps and Plates, size 16x22, illustrating the Natural Features of the Globe, the Geographical Distribution of Natural Phenomena, and their connection with the Industrial Pursuits of Mankind.

CONTENTS.

1. The World, illustrating the distribution of Land and Water, with the Contour and Comparative Relief of the Land.
2. Map of the World, showing the chief natural features and divisions of the Land, with the Ocean Currents.
3. Map showing the supposed Geological Structure of the Earth.
4. Map illustrating the Phenomena of Volcanic Action, showing the reaction of the interior of the Earth upon its external surface.
5. The Mountain-chains and River-systems of Europe.
6. The Mountain-chains and River-systems of Asia.
7. The Mountain-chains and River-systems of Africa.
8. The Mountain-chains and River-systems of North America.
9. The Mountain-chains and River-systems of South America.
10. Map of the World, illustrating the Climates of different regions, with the principal Hydrographic Basins of either Continent.
11. Co-tidal Lines and Curves of Equal Magnetic Variation.
12. Map of the World, illustrating the distribution of Vegetable Life in different regions, and as affected by conditions of climate.
13. Map of Botanical Regions, with the distribution and cultivation of all the important Plants used as food for Man.
14. Illustrations of the Perpendicular Distribution of Plants in the Torrid, Temperate, and Frigid Zones.
15. Map showing the Geographical Distribution of the principal Mammalia.
16. Illustrations of the Perpendicular Distribution of Animals in the Torrid, Temperate, and Frigid Zones.
17. Map showing the Geographical Distribution of Birds and Reptiles.
18. Map showing the Distribution of Mankind, according to the amount and comparative density of Population in different Lands; with the present distribution of Man according to Race, and the geographical distribution of the principal Religions.
19. Map illustrating the Natural Productions of different Lands, and the Principal Routes of Maritime Commerce.
20. Physical Map of the British Islands.

Imperial Quarto, handsomely bound in Cloth, gilt edges. Price, $4.50.

Educational and Geographical Works.

MAPS, CHARTS, DIAGRAMS.

BOSTON SCHOOL SUPPLY COMPANY,
Wholesale Educational Booksellers, Importers, and General School Furnishers,
JOHN A. BOYLE, Manager.   15 BROMFIELD STREET, BOSTON.

BOSTON SCHOOL SUPPLY CO.

HUGHES'
New Educational Wall Maps.

UNANIMOUSLY ADOPTED BY THE CITY OF BOSTON.

CITY OF BOSTON, DEPARTMENT OF PUBLIC INSTRUCTION,
Secretary's Office.

BOSTON SCHOOL SUPPLY CO.

Gentlemen,—At a meeting of the School Committee of Boston, held June 26th, the following order was passed by the Board on the recommendation of the Committee on Text Books:

ORDERED. That Hughes' Series of Maps be authorized for use in the Grammar Schools.

Yours very truly,   PHINEAS BATES,
Sec'y Sch. Committee.

DESCRIPTION.— Prepared expressly for School use under the personal supervision of William Hughes, F. R. G. S. Names introduced with great judgment, free from overcrowding. Physical features boldly and distinctly delineated. Political boundaries carefully colored. Adapted to any series of geographies.

MOUNTING.— On strong Cloth, with Rollers, Colored and Varnished. Size uniformly 54x68 inches.

Wholesale Price.

1. World on Mercator's Projection $6.00
2. World in Hemispheres 4.50
3. North America 4.50
4. South America 4.50
5. Europe 4.50
6. Asia 4.50
7. Africa 4.50
8. The United States, drawn from latest Government Surveys, just ready 4.50

SUPPLEMENTARY MAPS.
UNIFORM IN SIZE AND STYLE.

England and Wales 4.50
Scotland 4.50
Ireland 4.50
British Isles 6.00
Australia and New Zealand 4.50
Palestine 4.50

☞ ANY MAP SOLD SEPARATELY.

COLTON'S LIBRARY MAPS.

DESCRIPTION. — Engraving fine. Full in details. Railroads are shown; also all towns.

MOUNTING. — On Cloth — Rollers — Varnished.

1. The Eastern Hemisphere. 48x48 . . . . $7.00
2. The Western Hemisphere. 48x48 . . . . 7.00
3. United States, Mexico, Central America, and the West Indies. 72x80 . . . . 10.00
4. South America. 50x46 . . . . 7.00
5. Europe. 58x44 . . . . 7.00
6. Africa. 58x44 . . . . 7.00
7. Asia. 58x44 . . . . 7.00
8. Occanica. 48x60 . . . . 7.00

CLASSICAL MAPS.

COLTON'S.

DESCRIPTION. — In style of execution bold and clear. Nearly uniform in size. Embraces all names mentioned in text books.

1. The Roman Empire. 45x59 . . . . $5.00
2. Western Europe (Britannia, Gallia, Hispania, etc.). 59x40 . 5.00
3. Italy. 59x40 . . . . 5.00
4. Greece, Macedonia, etc. 59x40 . . . . 5.00
5. Asia Minor (including Thrace, Macedonia, Greece, Syria, Lower Egypt, etc.). 45x59 . . . . 5.00

JOHNSTON'S.

1. Orbis Veteribus Notus. 50x42 . . . . $3.50
2. Italia Antiqua. 50x42 . . . . 3.50
3. Græcia Antiqua. 50x42 . . . . 3.50
4. Asia Minor. 50x42 . . . . 3.50
5. Orbis Romanus. 50x42 . . . . 3.50

GUYOT'S.

1. The Roman Empire. 72x96 . . . . $12.50
2. Ancient Greece (including Ancient City of Athens). 72x96 . 12.50
3. Italia (including Map of Ancient Rome). 72x96 . . . . . 10.00

Johnston's Pictures for Schools.

USEFUL GRAINS. A Series of Pictures for Object Lessons. Beautifully drawn and printed in Colors. The Grains represented are:—

    BARLEY.   BUCKWHEAT.   MILLET.
    MAIZE.   OATS.   RICE.
    RYE.   WHEAT.

Each Picture represents the Plant twice the natural size, and is mounted on a strong board, 20 by 13 inches, and varnished. *Descriptive letter-press accompanies each Illustration.* Price $3.50.

USEFUL TREES. Trees grown for their Wood. Beautifully drawn and printed in Colors. Size of each drawing, 25 by 20 inches. Price, mounted on cotton with rollers, each 88c.

    THE OAK.   THE ELM.   THE FIR.
    THE BEECH.   THE MAHOGANY.   THE ASH.

A short description accompanies each Tree.

USEFUL PLANTS. A Series of Useful Plants, beautifully drawn and printed in Colors. Size of each drawing, 25 by 20 inches. Price, mounted on cotton, with rollers, each 88c.

    THE TEA PLANT.   THE COFFEE PLANT.
    THE SUGAR PLANT.   THE COTTON PLANT.
    THE COCOA PLANT.   THE TOBACCO PLANT.

A short description accompanies each Plant.

JOHNSTON'S ETHNOGRAPHICAL HEADS, "The Races of Mankind." Five Typical Heads, showing the distinguishing characteristics of the Caucasian, Mongolian, Indian, Malayan, and Negro Races; colored, life size, in one sheet. Size, 34 by 26 inches. On cloth and roller, varnished, $1.40.

JOHNSTON'S TYPES OF NATIONS. Size, 34 by 26 inches; on cloth and roller, varnished. Each $1.40.

    ESQUIMAUX.   NORTH AMERICAN INDIAN.
    NEGRO.   HINDOO.
    MALAY.   CHINESE.

BOSTON SCHOOL SUPPLY CO.

REYNOLDS'
PHILOSOPHICAL CHARTS.

This series of Charts will be found of great utility in imparting a correct knowledge of the Great Principles of Science. Each chart is complete in itself, and presents a Synopsis of the Science illustrated. The illustrations are boldly drawn, on a very large scale, and are well suited for viewing at a distance. Interesting and clear descriptive notes accompany each chart.

Chart 1. — **Laws of Matter and Motion.** Illustrating the Properties of Bodies, Laws of Gravitation, The Pendulum, Central Forces, Centrifugal Force, Centripetal Force, Laws of Motion, Angles of Incidence and Reflection, Composition and Resolution of Forces, etc. Size, 60 by 40 inches, on cloth, colored and varnished, with rollers. $3.75.

Chart 2. — **Mechanical Powers.** Illustrating the various kinds of Levers and their Applications, Wheel and Axle, Windlass, Capstan, Pulleys and their Combinations; The Inclined Plane and its Uses, The Wedge, Screws, and their Applications, etc. Size, 60 by 40 inches, on cloth, colored and varnished, with rollers. $3.75.

Chart 3. — **Principles of Hydrostatics.** Illustrating the Science of the Pressure and Equilibrium of Liquids, including the principles of Water Supply to Towns, Intermitting Springs, Syphons, Hydrostatic Balances, Laws of Floating Bodies, Hydrometers, Hydrostatic Press, etc. Size, 60 by 40 inches, on cloth, colored and varnished, with rollers. $3.75.

Chart 4. — **Principles of Hydraulics.** Illustrating the Science of Fluids in Motion, and the action of the various Machinery connected therewith, including Pumps, Water-Wheels, Water-Ram, Centrifugal Pump, Persian Wheel, Archimedian Screw, Fountains, etc. Size, 60 by 40 inches, on cloth, colored and varnished, with rollers. $3.75.

REYNOLDS' GEOGRAPHICAL CHART. Illustrating the principal subjects of Physical Geography, including the Physical Features of the Land, Movements of the Waters, including the Marine Currents, Tides, River Systems, etc., Distribution of the Winds, Monsoons, and Typhoons, Distribution of the Rain, Distribution of Climates, Volcanoes, Earthquake Regions, etc. On six sheets, each 30x20 inches, Colored, with Descriptive Notes.

    Complete in folio form $3.50
    Mounted on cloth, varnished, with rollers . . 5.60

REYNOLDS' ASTRONOMICAL CHART. Illustrating the principal phenomena of this sublime Science, boldly drawn and colored ; including the Solar System, Telescopic Views of the Sun and Moon, The Earth and its Atmosphere, The Seasons, Phases of the Moon, Eclipses of the Sun and Moon, Comparative Magnitudes of the Planets, Spring and Neap Tides, Phenomena of Day and Night, etc. On six sheets, each 25x20 inches, with Description.

    Complete in folio form $3.50
    Mounted on cloth, varnished, with rollers . . 5.25

REYNOLDS' ETHNOLOGICAL CHART. Fifty Full-length Figures, showing the Characteristic Features, Color, Height, and National Costumes of the principal Varieties of the Human Race. Correctly grouped and colored. On four sheets, each 30x20 inches, with Description by E. G. RAVENSTEIN, F.R.G.S.

    Complete in folio form $3.00
    Mounted on cloth, varnished, with rollers . . 4.67

REYNOLDS' GEOMETRICAL CHART. A series of Large Diagrams illustrating the Principles and Applications of Geometry, comprising Ninety-three Diagrams, boldly drawn and colored, including the Trigonometrical Circle and its parts, Lines and Angles, Triangles, Quadrangles, Circulars, Polygons, Prisms, Pyramids, Spheres, and other Solids, Conic Sections, Curves, Euclid's famous 47th Proposition, Measurement of Areas, Heights, Distances, etc. Four sheets, each 30 by 20 inches, Colored, with Explanatory Notes,

    Complete in folio form $2.00
    Mounted on cloth, varnished, with rollers, 3.67

REYNOLDS' BOTANICAL CHART. Exhibiting the Structure, Physiology, and Classification of Plants. The Diagrams are boldly drawn and colored, and form an easy and pleasing method of teaching the Principles of Botany. On six sheets, with Description by JAMES STEWART.

    Complete in folio form $3.50
    Mounted on cloth, varnished, with rollers, 5.25

REYNOLDS' CHEMICAL CHART. Illustrating the Principles of Chemistry, and by means of which a comprehensive knowledge of this great Science may be easily taught and acquired without the aid of apparatus. The illustrations include Chemical Physics, the Nature of Elements, Compounds, Affinity, Acids, Bases, Salts, Isomerism, Chemistry of Food, Chemistry of Light, Combustion and Illumination; Chemistry of Animal and Vegetable Life, and the Utilization of their several products; Geological and Agricultural Chemistry, etc. On six sheets, each 25 by 20 inches, Colored, with Descriptive Notes,

    Complete in folio form $3.50
    Mounted on cloth, varnished, with rollers, 5.25

REYNOLDS' ZOOLOGICAL CHART. A series of Diagrams presenting a comprehensive view of the Animal Kingdom, from the highest to the lowest grades, comprising One Hundred and Thirteen Colored Illustrative Types of the various Classes and Orders of Animals. Drawn by WILLIAM SMART. On four sheets, each 30x20 inches, with Explanatory Notes.

  Complete in folio form $3.00
  Mounted on cloth, varnished, with rollers . . 4.67

REYNOLDS' GEOLOGICAL CHART. New Edition. Showing the Order of Succession of the Stratified Rocks, with their Mineral Characters, Principal Characteristic Fossils, Thickness, Localities, Uses in the Arts, etc. By JOHN MORRIS, F.G.S., Professor of Geology and Mineralogy in University College, London. This important chart has lately been revised by Prof. Morris, and the New Edition forms the most recent and complete Geological Synopsis extant. On a sheet 3 feet by 2 feet, Colored.

  In folio form $1.00
  Mounted on cloth, varnished, with rollers . . 1.60

REYNOLDS' ASTRONOMICAL GEOGRAPHY. A series of boldly executed and Colored Diagrams, illustrative of the Celestial Sphere, the Earth's position in space, Revolution of the Earth round the Sun, Latitude and Longitude explained, etc. Size — 4 feet 6 inches by 3 feet.

  Mounted on cloth, varnished, with rollers . . $3.50

www.ingramcontent.com/pod-product-compliance
Lightning Source LLC
Chambersburg PA
CBHW031119160426
43192CB00008B/1049